Are You a Candidate to Read This Book?

Take our quiz to find out. Simply mark Y for Yes or N for No on the line before each entry.

About You

___ I'm overwhelmed, overbooked, and overstressed, yet I take on more.

___ Some days I wonder where my dreams went.

___ It's hard for me to let go of grudges or my past.

___ I find it difficult to be happy for those who succeed.

___ I tend to lose the same ten pounds over and over and over.

___ I promise myself I'll say no but still find myself saying yes.

___ Everyone seems to do better than me.

___ I find it difficult to confront others with things they've done wrong—whether at home, at work, or with friends.

___ It isn't easy for me to make or keep friends.

___ Life isn't anything like my dreams . . . and I'm disappointed.

___ I feel bitter and angry sometimes, like I got the raw end of a deal.

___ I don't feel like what I do is very important.

___ Many of the things I do go unnoticed by others.

___ Some days I think, *I'm never going anywhere, am I? I'm just stuck.*

About Others

___ Others rarely (or never) listen to me, even when I have something important to say.

___ Others drop the ball a lot. I always end up picking it up and running with it to the finish line. Otherwise the task won't get done.

___ My sister/brother was "the perfect one" at home.

___ When others get angry, I freeze or go into super-pleaser mode.

___ Others don't give me much respect.

___ My parents were always hard on me. I couldn't do anything right.

___ I'm a cup-half-empty kind of person. I get down on myself a lot.

___ My family and/or co-workers take me and everything I do for granted.

___ Others act (or have acted) abusively toward me, whether in words or actions, and I just take it.

___ Every relationship I have seems to go wrong somewhere.

___ I find myself thinking, *Why can't I be more like her?*

If any of these topics resonated with you and you marked even one Y, you need to not only read this book but *carry it around with you.*

This book will scratch where you itch.

I promise.

Have a new you by Friday? Is it possible?

To tell you the truth, it's a scam. You can have a new you by *Wednesday* if you do just a few simple things. And then you can have an even *better* you by Friday! Keep reading, and I'll show you how.

This is the miracle turnaround you're looking for.

I guarantee it.

Have a
New You
by Friday

Have a
New You
by Friday

How to **A**ccept Yourself,
Boost Your Confidence &
Change Your Life in **5 Days**

Dr. Kevin Leman

Revell
a division of Baker Publishing Group
Grand Rapids, Michigan

Published by Revell
a division of Baker Publishing Group
P.O. Box 6287, Grand Rapids, MI 49516-6287
www.revellbooks.com

Printed in the United States of America

Library of Congress Cataloging-in-Publication Data
Leman, Kevin.
    Have a new you by Friday : how to accept yourself, boost your confidence &
change your life in 5 days / Kevin Leman.
        p.   cm.
    Includes bibliographical references.
    ISBN 978-0-8007-1933-3 (cloth)
    ISBN 978-0-8007-3424-4 (pbk.)
    1. Self-actualization—Religious aspects—Christianity. 2. Self-acceptance—
Religious aspects—Christianity. 3. Self-confidence—Religious aspects—
Christianity. I. Title.
BV4598.2.L46 2010
158.1—dc22   2010013619

To protect the privacy of those who have shared their stories with the author, some
details and names have been changed.

10   11   12   13   14   15   16   7   6   5   4   3

In keeping with biblical principles of
creation stewardship, Baker Publishing Group advocates the responsible
use of our natural resources. As a
member of the Green Press Initiative,
our company uses recycled paper
when possible. The text paper of
this book is comprised of 30% post-
consumer waste.

Contents

Wednesday

Thursday

Friday

Acknowledgments

With grateful thanks to my editorial power team:

Lonnie Hull DuPont, who always entertains my entrepreneurial ideas and maintains her sense of humor. (Besides that, she's never hung up on me and never told me I was wacko.)

Jessica Miles, my eagle-eyed Revell project editor, who can spot a grammatical flaw from a hundred paces.

Ramona Cramer Tucker, who can translate Leman-speak better than anyone else. You are appreciated.

Introduction

This Book Ought to Cost $199

How would you like "the new you" delivered? UPS, FedEx? (US mail is available, but at a slightly higher rate.) Or would you like the new you delivered via personal courier? With Kevin Leman, it's "satisfaction guaranteed!"

If you could change one thing about yourself, what would it be?

"Well, Dr. Leman," you're saying, "I could think of a bunch of things. How on earth could I pick just one?"

Congratulations! You're the very person I wrote this book for. You see, there's a reason you picked up this book. You'd like to see a few things—or many—change in your life. You may have tried other ways of helping this change along—asking a friend to hold you accountable, going to see a shrink, writing in a journal, counting to ten before you do the thing that gets you in trouble every time, etc. But have they worked? Nope. Or you would have "fixed yourself" and you wouldn't need this book.

How many times have you committed to say no to something you know you'll be asked to do . . . then found yourself signing up anyway? How many diets have you gone on in the last five or ten years (or more)? How many times have you lost the same ten pounds? (By modest calculation, then, someone like me has lost over 750 pounds in his lifetime.) How many times have you told yourself, *I'll never say that to my kids*, then not only do you say it, but you say it with the same tone your mom or dad used with you? How many times have you felt like a gerbil in a cage, running around and around on that wheel but never really going anywhere, never accomplishing anything?

> *There's a reason you picked up this book. You'd like to see a few things—or many— change in your life.*

If you can relate, *Have a New You by Friday* is for you. Thousands of families are finding help in *Have a New Kid by Friday* (there's no better "cure" for kids' unruly, disrespectful behavior than the secrets in that book) and in *Have a New Husband by Friday* (watch marriages—even those destined for divorce courts—transform in just five days). Now, *voila!* A five-day action plan that will change *your* life.

If you don't want to change your life, put this book back on the shelf now. Otherwise you'll just be adding it to your stack of other self-help books for kindling on a cold evening.

So what does it take from you? The willingness to do a little detective work in figuring out, *Just who am I? What makes me do what I do?*

Did you know that every day you tell yourself lies about who you are? That you act on those lies? That those lies affect how you treat yourself and the kinds of relationships you have with others? Now's the time to nip that lie-telling in the bud and bring the truth to light—for your own sake as well as for those you love.

Will this be easy? No, because we usually want to change other people before we think of changing ourselves. (Why do you think

Have a New Kid by Friday and *Have a New Husband by Friday* have become bestsellers? Ah, now you're getting it. . . .) And somehow it's much more difficult to change ourselves. But nothing good is ever accomplished without a little hard work (or did you miss that class in elementary school?).

Take, for instance, Dr. Evan O'Neill Kane, a former chief surgeon at Summit Hospital in New York City. He knew all about hard work. A pioneer in the medical profession in the late 1800s and the early 1900s, he had seen too many deaths and disabilities caused by general anesthesia. So he was convinced that most operations could and should be done under local anesthesia (where the patient is awake during the entire procedure).

> *Did you know that every day you tell yourself lies about who you are? That you act on those lies?*

But Dr. Kane had a problem—he didn't have any volunteers for this type of surgery. He spent a long time searching for just the right patient to try out his new procedure, but everyone was nervous (and rightly so) about being a guinea pig.

Finally, a patient volunteered to undergo the operation. On February 15, 1921, Dr. Kane performed this surgery for the first time. He removed the patient's appendix in the operating room. Amazingly, the patient recovered so quickly that he was released from the hospital two days after surgery—an unheard-of event in the early 1900s.[1] It was a milestone success in the medical field.

Why did Dr. Kane succeed? Because he didn't let a few road bumps stop him. Because he believed there was a better way, a safer way, to do surgery, with less risk to the patient. He realized that, with a little bit of pain (local anesthesia versus general anesthesia), the patient would be better off in the long run.

In the same way, there's some pain involved with becoming a new you by Friday. In fact, I was tempted to call this book *Have a New You by Saturday Night* because I know how difficult it is to change yourself. It's a little like trying to rub the spots off a leopard with a Brillo pad.

My goal this year is to see the tips of my shoes. I haven't seen them in years. (Of course, my expanding waistline could have something to do with the "little slices" of Marie Callender's pie I find myself sneaking from the refrigerator when my wife isn't looking.) I know how stubborn and set in my ways I am. Change doesn't come easy. Can you relate?

> *I know how difficult it is to change yourself. My goal this year is to see the tips of my shoes. I haven't seen them in years.*

But could the reason it's so hard to change have something to do with the lies we're telling ourselves—*about* ourselves?

Have a New You by Friday will take you to some areas about yourself that might be a little uncomfortable for a bit. But it's the good kind of hurt that will propel you forward rather than keep you stuck in the rut that frustrates you. All of us have things we'd like to change about ourselves. So why not step up to the plate to become the person you want to be? Tell yourself, *This time I'm really going to do it. No excuses. No holding back. I want to be different. I want my relationships to be different.*

So why not take control of your life now? Instead of your paying a shrink $225 per session to listen to you whine about your life, I'll walk you through your own personal clinic. You'll come to understand your personality; the secret forces that influence you to say, think, and act as you do; and how you can best accept and give love to improve your relationships. This isn't one of those touchy-feely books that lets you "glow" for an hour about yourself . . . and then the next day you find yourself right back where you were. No, this is the life-changing makeover you'll want to tell all of your friends about (even that cousin you don't like).

So why not put yourself in the driver's seat of having a new you? After all, there's no one who knows you like you. There's no unnecessary waiting. No endless insurance forms to fill out. No hefty charges on your Visa bill at the end of the month. You're going to walk away with such great stuff that you won't be able to wait for tomorrow to start so you can show off the new you.

Why not live life the way you really want to? Don't let the lies you're telling yourself hold you back. Today's the day. You're in charge of the new you.

I'll teach you how to

> *Tell yourself,* This time I'm really going to do it. No excuses. No holding back. I want to be different. I want my relationships to be different.

- accept the truth about yourself;
- boost your confidence by identifying the lies you're telling yourself . . . and putting them to rest for good;
- change your life by concentrating on becoming who you *really* want to be.

And all that in just five days.

That's why this book ought to cost $199. Then you'd still have $26 left over in your pocket (instead of going to that $225 appointment with the shrink) to go out and do something fun to celebrate the emerging new you.

Why not experience that rush of accomplishment you've been waiting for? You can be a better person by Tuesday, have an enlarged perspective by Wednesday, have a new drive by Thursday, and become your own shrink by Friday—all by doing just a few simple things.

The Road Map to a New You

On Monday, we'll discover who you really are—and how to use that knowledge to your own best advantage. What kind of personality do you have? And how do these traits affect you and the ones you love? Why is it that families are rather diverse—with a host of personality differences—even though all the children come from the same mold?

On Tuesday, we'll look at the family you grew up in—and how your place in that "zoo" influenced you more than you might guess. Did you know that a good bit of your life script was written for you based on decisions made by your parents? (That doesn't really sound fair, does it? But I'll show you why it's true. How many kids your parents have, what order they had them in, how they treated you, etc., have everything to do with what makes you "you"—and with the areas in which you succeed and the areas in which you fail.) You can't fully understand yourself without understanding the family dynamics in which you were raised.

> *Why not live life the way you really want to?*

On Wednesday, we'll uncover the lies you're telling yourself (none of you is immune from those nasty tapes playing in your head), how they impact you, and what you can do about them. Early childhood memories provide the key to unlocking the mystery of why you see things the way you do, why certain things bug you that don't bug others, and why some things comfort you that frighten others. They reveal your unspoken assumptions about the way you think life ought to go . . . and not go.

On Thursday, we'll talk about love. No, not the kind of gushy romance that makes couples all googly-eyed at each other, but the way in which each of us gives love and receives love. Understanding more about the styles of love will smooth potential road bumps and help you succeed in interpersonal connections.

On Friday, you get to be your own shrink, free of charge. I'll show you how to use what you've learned to become the expert on yourself—and to guarantee the new you for a lifetime.

A Little Pain, Great Gain

Remember the story about Dr. Evan O'Neill Kane, who performed that milestone surgery? Well, here's the kicker: the patient who volunteered for the experimental surgery was Dr. Kane himself! Yes, Dr. Kane actually took out his own appendix on the operating table.[2] He's living proof that you can do anything if you try, and that a little pain can bring great gain—for yourself and for your loved ones.

Through *Have a New You by Friday*, you'll discover your strengths and weaknesses, your biases, and your basic assumptions about life (including how and why they sometimes clash with the assumptions of those you spend time with), and be able to draw your own road map for relational success. After all, if you know who you are, you'll know how to improve those areas that have held you back. Then there will be nothing to hold you back. You'll have a newfound determination to live life as you really want to.

I can't wait to watch you fly.

Monday

Just Who Do You Think You Are?
(You Might Be Surprised)

What's your real personality, and how did you get to be that way?
And why settle for less when you can be so much more?

Have you ever seen the hilarious *Bob Newhart Show*? I used to love watching the show in its original run and sometimes catch the reruns now on Nick at Nite. Bob Newhart, a psychologist, always held intriguing small group sessions with his needy clients. My favorite episode is one where a man named Mr. Peterson had a job as a salesman, but he wasn't doing very well. He wasn't selling anything, so he dragged himself to Bob Newhart's session and asked Bob if he could help figure out the problem.

Bob asked Mr. Peterson to describe what he did on a sales call.

"Well," Mr. Peterson said, "I go to the door. If no one opens the door, I go to the next door."

After more digging, Bob was astounded to find out that Mr. Peterson feared failure so much that he never even *knocked* on any of the doors! No wonder he wasn't making any sales!

But isn't that what a lot of us do? We spend life standing at closed doors, not risking knocking, because we fear what might happen if we really try. We get stuck in a rut because we fear hearing "no" and having a door slammed in our face.

> **Lies You Tell Yourself**
>
> I can't do it, so I might as well not try.
> I can't do it right, so I might as well not try.
> So-and-so can do it better, so I might as well not try.

I ought to know, because that was the story of my life, until a gray-haired lady, Miss Wilson, got ahold of me.

I was one of those kids going nowhere in life—and taking his time to get there. If it weren't for three even more hapless bottom-dwellers, I would have graduated dead last in my high school class. Everyone, including me, pretty much figured that Kevin Leman would spend his entire career fixing flats and changing tires at the local gas station, selling newspapers at a street corner kiosk, or maybe even picking up trash alongside the road.

To be honest, I thought I was dumber than mud. And I acted like it too.

Then one almost magical day in April of 1961, when I was 17, I had a conversation with a math teacher that changed my life.

> *If it weren't for three even more hapless bottom-dwellers, I would have graduated dead last in my high school class.*

Miss Wilson was an old woman, somewhere between estrogen and death, her gray hair just on the verge of turning blue. She had seen thousands of students come and go through her school, including my perfect sister, Sally, and my "Mr. Most Likely to Succeed" brother, Jack, and she cornered me after one of my many "incidents."

You see, I was a creative master of classroom incidents. One of my favorite activities was doing obscene birdcalls in class. I could get away with talking like a sailor because I did it like I was imitating a bird, so you had to listen carefully to hear that I was actually saying something dirty or making fun of the teacher. The teacher, of course, was usually trying to ignore me, leaving her no time to interpret my calls, so I had a field day making some of the students around me grab their sides in laughter.

If verbal humor didn't put me in the spotlight, I tried being a master performance artist. I carved out a spot in a book for a water pistol so I could spray classmates without them knowing where it came from. I set a fire in a classroom garbage can so we'd get out of a test. And I successfully crawled out of history class on my hands and knees without the teacher even noticing I was gone. It was a tremendous piece of work, if I may say so myself.

"Why would you *do* that?" some of you might be asking, and that's a fair question. The fact is, I didn't escape in order to sneak down the hall to get a candy bar from the snack machine or to smoke in the boys' room. I didn't even particularly want to leave the class—after all, they were a good audience. I just craved attention and would do almost anything for a laugh. I'd raised the bar so high that to keep getting attention, I had to keep doing even more bizarre things. No wonder that due to my antics, one of my teachers resigned not only from teaching at my school but from the entire teaching profession.

I'd raised the bar so high that to keep getting attention, I had to keep doing even more bizarre things.

Spunky Miss Wilson had seen enough. She finally cornered me a few months before graduation. "Kevin, I know you and I know your family. I've watched you over the years."

Here it comes, I thought. *Another lecture asking me why I can't be more like my brother or sister.*

But Miss Wilson went in an entirely different direction. "You know, it occurred to me the other day, and I wonder if it ever occurred to you, that maybe you could use some of the energy you expend on these antics to really make something of yourself, rather than just being the proverbial class clown—at your expense, I would add."

What shocked me about this conversation was that Miss Gray Hair wasn't just telling me off like the other teachers did. She actually saw something good in me. Sure, it was obvious she saw this jerky little show-off, the baby of the family, putting on another embarrassing performance. But instead of seeing a loser, she saw potential. And she had enough insight to challenge me by suggesting I could do something with my life. I didn't have to be a slave to the worst tendencies of my personality.

As I look back on my life and count the people who have really mattered, Miss Wilson is in the top five. If it hadn't been for her, you might have been reading *about* me (in the police blotter section of your newspaper), but you probably wouldn't be picking up a book written *by* me.

But what made me so eager to grab attention when I was young?

The answer is simple: I had nowhere else to go.

Perfect Sally and My Brother, "God"

Have you ever been around an every-hair-in-place, ever-competent, always trustworthy, and thoroughly dependable person? The kind of person who makes you feel unworthy to even breathe next to her? That was my perfect firstborn sister, Sally.

Sally was the kind of student who always told her girlfriends, "I think I really blew the

---

Who's Important to You?

What three or four people in your life have influenced you the most? What role have they played in your life, and how would you describe their personality traits?

Person #1:
Role in your life:
Personality traits:

Person #2:
Role in your life:
Personality traits:

Person #3:
Role in your life:
Personality traits:

Person #4:
Role in your life:
Personality traits:

How many of these people did you describe in a positive way?

How many did you describe in a negative way?

---

test," then found out she got "only" 97 percent on it. Eight years older than me, Sally was in many ways like a second mother. I saw no flaws in her. If Jesus hadn't been born yet, I think Sally could have been a pretty good candidate for Mary's role. That's how highly I esteemed her.

My brother, Jack—whom I not so affectionately referred to as "God"—was to guys what Sally was to girls. He'd cornered the market on success: quarterback of the football team, a strong student, handsome and popular, very well liked, and never lacking for a date. Jack had all the confidence of the oldest son.

Then there was me. Little lastborn Cubby, Kevin Leman. Where did I fit in that perfect mix of my siblings? I couldn't be a better student than Sally—that was obvious. I didn't have Jack's athletic prowess—that was also obvious. Compared to him, I always felt scrawny (of course, he was older than me, but you don't think like that when you're a kid). There was no room for me to get noticed by being an excellent student or a class leader. So I realized somewhere deep down that if I wanted attention, I'd have to look elsewhere, because Sally and Jack had covered all the positive bases.

> *From behind my biased eyes, there was no way to gain notoriety except by being a cutup.*

From behind my biased eyes, there was no way to gain notoriety except by being a cutup. I wasn't a mean-spirited kid (though many of my teachers would probably beg to differ, having experienced so much frustration with my antics). Rather, my goal was to make people laugh. If it put me on center stage, so much the better.

My love of laughter came almost by accident. I was in second grade, eight years old, when Sally recruited me to be the mascot on her cheerleading squad. One time, in the middle of a game, I totally messed up a cheer. Initially I was embarrassed, but when I looked up into that sea of faces, watching everyone point at me and laugh, I remember thinking, *Hey, this isn't so bad*, and I even milked it a little bit. Doing so wasn't conscious. I was too young for that. But the desire to make a mark, to be noticed, to become someone, is ingrained in each of us, and I knew I had somehow found my niche at last: I would spend my life making people laugh.

And guess who was watching all this develop? My gray-haired math teacher, Miss Wilson. She recognized me as a people person. She saw how I manipulated my mother (who seemingly spent more time in school than I did, trying to get me out of the problems I created), and she realized that my creative powers of persuasion could be put to nobler uses.

> *Most of the kids loved having me in their class. As soon as they realized I'd be in their homeroom, they'd whisper to each other, "Oh, good, we've got Leman! This is gonna be a fun year!"*

It's not that I hadn't been lectured before, but all my teachers had said the same thing: "If Kevin would just apply himself, he could do so much better." I'd simply shrug, because I already knew my answer. Why apply myself with hard work when I knew I couldn't do as well as my siblings—and I could have so much fun entertaining everyone? The fact that the teachers didn't like me didn't bother me one bit; most of the kids loved having me in their class. As soon as they realized I'd be in their homeroom, they'd whisper to each other, "Oh, good, we've got Leman! This is gonna be a fun year!"

At first it bothered me that this old biddy could see through me, but then something in her eyes stopped me. Her expression told me she saw something that no one else did and that I ought to give her a chance. So, even though I still thought I was dumber than mud, I agreed that she could tutor me my senior year, from April through June. "If you work a little harder, you still might graduate," she assured me.

So work I did—for perhaps the first time in my life. No one was more amazed by this than me. Miss Wilson was a great teacher; I just had been too busy with my antics to notice that before. And you know what? I really wanted to please her—and that was a new experience for Kevin Leman.

Our efforts paid off. I flunked only one class that semester— a record for me. (Whereas my mom expected all As and an occasional B from my brother and sister, she got on her knees to pray that I could pull off the occasional C, just to reassure herself that, in her words, "God didn't forget to put a brain in that boy.")

I'll never forget the afternoon I walked up to the posted list at school that carried the names of all the seniors who would be graduating the next day. There was my name, bigger than life. Now *I* was the one laughing.

Well, Leman, I said to myself, *you did it. You're going to be a high school graduate. You may never accomplish anything else in your life, but this is something you actually got done.*

That Was Just the Beginning of My New Start

After a little ingenuity, and lots of letter writing (uh, make that *begging*), I finally convinced a college to accept me. When I look back, that was truly a miracle, since my academic records were so bad.

Not only did I get into college, but I continually surprised myself. I started to succeed, although it might be different from what you'd consider success. I'll never forget looking at that first college report card: I saw all Cs and just one D. While such a report card would have horrified my sister, it made me feel tremendous. For the first time in my life I was getting Cs. I remember thinking, *That means for the most part I'm doing average college work— that's pretty good.*

But interestingly, this new "successful" Kevin Leman took some getting used to. I wasn't comfortable with him. I'd never seen myself as successful, so it took some time to adjust my perceptions.

The second trimester I did about the same, except that I got an A in baseball. Then, in my third trimester, I ran into kinesiology (or better said, kinesiology ran into me). At that point in my life, I was considering becoming a PE teacher. After all, gym teachers could be dumber than mud and still survive, right? I loved sports and thought, *If they want to pay me for being in charge of seven hours of recreation, that's not a bad gig.*

> *I'd never seen myself as successful, so it took some time to adjust my perceptions.*

Unfortunately, the old Kevin kept resurrecting himself, and the school threw me out for a prank that a dean took a little too seriously. Out of options, I went home to live with my parents in Tucson, Arizona.

Picture this: I was 19 years old, thrown out of college, with not much hope for the future. I was glad to at least get a job as a janitor in a medical center. For the next five years I worked there, thinking that all my teachers were right: I wasn't going much of anywhere, so I might as well get used to it.

I was stuck in my rut.

"She Believes in Me"

Something amazing happened while I worked as a janitor.

Have you ever heard the old Kenny Rogers song "She Believes in Me"? I'm the living testimony to the power of those lyrics. First, my math teacher Miss Wilson believed in me. She was convinced that I could be more than a show-off, that I had something special I could give the world. And because of her, I went to college (even if it didn't work out at first . . . but wait, more on that coming).

Then I met Sande, a beautiful young woman who watered the seeds sown by Miss Wilson. When she saw me in the medical center, she didn't see "just the janitor." She saw *me*—Kevin Leman. And evidently she liked what she saw enough, or at least was too kind to turn me down, so she agreed to go out on a date with me, even if it was only sharing a 20-cent cheeseburger, since that's all the money I had in my pocket at the time.

Sande—the first-class woman who believed in me and what I could accomplish—became my inspiration.

I continued to work as a janitor but also went back to college part-time, this time to the University of Arizona . . . and I flunked the same course twice. Normally, looking at that F—twice—would have sent me back into my usual rut, thinking, *Who am I trying to kid? This academic stuff just isn't for me.*

But this time I had someone who believed in me—Sande (later, in the field behind my parents' home, she even agreed to be my wife . . . yes, I was even dumb as mud in the area of romance)—and continually encouraged me to do better. I refused to give in to my old patterns of failure. I worked harder and studied longer. When I finally got into the university full-time, I was practically dumbfounded by my first report card: all As except for one B, which qualified me for the dean's list.

> **Got Guts?**
>
> Ask yourself:
> 1. Am I stuck in a rut? If so, what one(s)?
> 2. Do I fear change? Fear success? Fear becoming someone different, even though I long to be different? Why?
> 3. What self-improvement techniques have I tried before? Why did they not work?
>
> Tell yourself, *This time, I'm going to do what I need to do. Five days and I'll be a new person. Look out, world!*

> *I refused to give in to my old patterns of failure. I worked harder and studied longer.*

I remember reading my name out loud from that sheet of paper—"Kevin Leman, on the dean's list"—with mixed feelings. Yes, I was proud of the grades I'd worked so hard to earn, but I also struggled with disbelief. The grades were totally inconsistent with how I saw myself. I wasn't sure how to reconcile the new Kevin Leman with the old Kevin Leman I knew so well.

> *I wasn't sure how to reconcile the new Kevin Leman with the old Kevin Leman I knew so well.*

The next semester, I was on the dean's list again. After that, I received a notice in the mail from the university, telling me I had received university scholarship honors. They were actually going to pay me to finish college! Talk about shock. But since I earned minimum wage as a janitor, I couldn't help but be thrilled.

How My Life Changed

Dr. Leman, I'll never forget the story you told about your childhood at a seminar in Texas. I could relate. I've always felt "dumber than mud"—and I was always the fat girl everyone picked on too. So I tried to make everyone laugh instead.

Later I got into a design job with a comics firm so I could make people laugh and get paid to do it. I've done really well in that career, believe it or not. But I've also spent 42 years feeling bad about myself and probably a thousand bucks or more on self-improvement books. Nothing helped . . . until I heard you. For the first time I realized I've been blaming other people for the way they treated me growing up (my dad was super critical; my mom died when I was eight). But all along it's been *me* who's been my own worst enemy. That day I spent an hour sobbing in the bathroom at that conference center, but I walked out with a determination to do things differently, to stop putting myself down.

It's been three months since I made that promise to myself. Things haven't changed instantly (now, wouldn't that be nice?), but I'm a different person. My co-workers have noticed that something's going on because I'm standing up for myself more. I don't feel like I always have to be "the funny one." (That performance track was getting really old.) Thanks for the wake-up call.

Maria, Texas

The next few years only widened the gap between who I had perceived myself to be in the past and who I was becoming. I became a member of Psy Chi, a national honor society for psychology students. Later, I shocked myself even further by getting into a master's program with relative ease, and then even went on to get a doctorate degree. As I would have said when I was a high school student, "Who would have ever thunk it?"

And now you're reading a book written by a guy who was going nowhere but who somehow ended up getting at least a few things done. Why? It all started because someone believed in me.

Who believes in you? What person in your life has played—or could play—the role of a Miss Wilson or a Sande?

> *Who believes in you? What person in your life has played—or could play—the role of a Miss Wilson or a Sande?*

Why Be Less When You Can Be More?

Remember Mr. Peterson, who couldn't make a sale because he was so afraid of failure that he didn't even knock on the door?

Consider this: not even the best salesman in the world is going to get a yes every time. And he will have plenty of doors slammed in his face as he tries. But how do you know if you can do something unless you try?

Most likely you've tried a few things along the way to become a new you. You've tried . . . and failed. This time it's going to be different. In just five days, if you follow the principles in this book, *you will become a new you.* Now that's exciting!

But it's also a little scary, right? After all, being in a rut is sometimes a lot more comfortable. To make any change, you have to decide you want to make that change and be willing to do the work it requires to get there.

> *To make any change, you have to decide you want to make that change and be willing to do the work it requires to get there.*

Remember Dr. Evan O'Neill Kane, the surgeon who performed an appendectomy on himself? Well, that's what this chapter is all about—taking a look inward at your personality and what makes you "you," and doing a little operation on yourself. Can it be done? Yes. Will it be difficult? Probably. But maybe not as much as you think. And I guarantee that, by Tuesday and Wednesday, you'll be amazed at the progress you've made. You'll understand yourself better and why you think and respond the way you do.

Your Secrets Revealed

The very fact that you picked up a book with the title *Have a New You by Friday* tells me some things about you.

You're interested in finding out more about what makes you the way you are. Maybe you've always wondered why you're so very different from your siblings—after all, you grew up in the same house and had the same parents (or at least shared one of the parents), but you probably represent opposite points on the personality scale. Maybe you're the Sally in your family. Or the Jack. Or Cubby Leman, like me.

Why is that?

In short, you want to know what kind of personality you have— is it a "good" personality, a winning personality, or a destructive personality?

But the mere fact that you're asking that question shows me you have another aim in mind—you're wondering if you might be able to use this book to *improve* your personality. Maybe you wish you could be more outgoing, more comfortable in social situations, or more confident. Maybe you are tired of letting others run all over you while you do the work. Maybe you've been told you have a grating personality or you're too controlling.

In other words, you'd like to be a completely different you.

Have you ever seen one of the makeovers on *Oprah*, when a couple women with straight hair, drab clothing, and poorly applied makeup come onstage and admit, "I need a change. What I've got just isn't working"? Forty minutes later, after some careful attention from makeup artists, hair stylists, and clothing experts, these same women walk out looking like models—or at least attractive anchorwomen. The change is impressive indeed.

Well, I'm convinced that personality makeovers are just as possible as appearance makeovers because I've seen them happen over and over in the lives of real people.

People like you.

The first step toward changing your personality or behavior is to identify what your personality really is (you may think you know, but you may be very surprised!), and why, as a result, you act the way you do.

The second step is deciding what aspect(s) of that personality you want to change. For example, "I'd like to be more extroverted." "I'd like to have more friends." "I don't want to be boring." "I need to say no without feeling guilty."

Most of us are operating in personality ruts that have been forged over the years, and getting out of a rut isn't easy. Just ask Bryant Gumbel.

In 1999, after fifteen years of working on the *Today* show at NBC, Gumbel started hosting CBS's *The Early Show*. For fifteen years, Gumbel had made countless transitions into commercials by saying, "This is *Today* on NBC." Now he was on a new show with a new network. Old habits die hard. During his first week on the air, the inevitable happened. While on *The Early Show*, Gumbel fell back into old patterns and welcomed his viewers by saying, "This is *Today* on NBC."

There was an awkward silence, a little laughter, and the show carried on. Steve Friedman, the producer, was sympathetic toward Gumbel's miscue. "You say something four or five times a day for fifteen years, and it's kind of hard to break. I figure Bryant said it 15,000 times at *Today*; now make it 15,001."[1]

All of us have these same ruts, don't we? We may not be on camera, but we've conditioned ourselves to say and do things and to respond in certain ways that have become so second nature we don't even think about them.

> *The goal of this book is to get you to think outside the box you've put yourself in.*

The goal of this book is to get you to think outside the box you've put yourself in. To rethink everything you've been doing, all the assumptions you hold about yourself, and even the rule book you live by. Surprise—bet some of you didn't even know you have a rule book, but it's there, and it's controlling your life. For some of you, it's ruining your life. (More on this on Wednesday.)

As you become a new you, you'll learn how to identify and build on your natural strengths (mine being an outgoing guy who loves to help others through the gifts of inspiration, entertainment, and commonsense wisdom) rather than try to create an artificial personality (mine being a class clown who could only think up annoying antics because I couldn't figure out what else to be or where else to make my mark on the planet). You'll also learn how to think through, and nip in the bud, the hidden lies you believe about yourself that keep you from accomplishing your goals and enjoying relationships.

I wasted so many years by selling myself short, by not believing in myself, by always saying to myself, "My brother or sister could do that, but I can't. So why try?"

But look what can happen when you decide that today's the day—the day you're going to start on your path to a new you!

Who would have believed 40 years ago that Kevin Leman could even *read* over 35 books, much less write them? Leman books have killed an entire forest of trees—they're printed in 18 different languages. My seminars have been attended by hundreds of thousands, and I've spoken to millions on radio and television. I don't say this boastfully, but with utter astonishment, knowing my background and weaknesses as well as I do.

Once you really understand yourself—your personality, your strengths and weaknesses, your predispositions, your family background, the sneaky lies you believe, and how you best give and receive love—there will be no holding you back. You can climb vocational mountains, break out of relational ruts, and forge new social patterns. You can be the new you you've always longed to be.

It all starts with identifying your personality, because it says so much about who you are and how you respond to life's challenges.

The Four Temperaments: Which One Is Most "You"?

It's a well-known fact that all of us have a temperament, and temperaments run the gamut from the laid-back, water-off-the-duck's-back personality to the every-moment-is-a-crisis personality.

Temperaments have been around for a long time. In fact, more than two thousand years ago, a smart gentleman named Hippocrates organized the temperaments into four basic categories (sanguine, choleric, melancholic, phlegmatic) by connecting them with bodily "humors." Here's a quick rundown of his thoughts.

Popular Sanguines

Blood was associated with a sanguine personality—laughter, music, a passionate disposition.[2] Leman translation: Sanguines are the fun-loving types who are always eager to explore, experience new things, and just enjoy the day.

Powerful Cholerics

Yellow bile represented a person quick to anger or *choleric* (meaning yellow).[3] Leman translation: Cholerics are those who want to get things done "just right," which means their own way.

Perfect Melancholies

Black bile represented a depressed personality—*melan* meaning "black."[4] Leman translation: Melancholies are those who see the grass as always greener on the other side of the fence but don't have the get-up-and-go to check it out. They're like Garfield the cat, who's always lying around saying, "I should do this or that. . . . No, guess I'll do it tomorrow."

Peaceful Phlegmatics

Phlegm represented someone with a phlegmatic personality— sluggish and dull.[5] Leman translation: Phlegmatics are the peace-makers who just want everyone to get along and don't want to ruffle anyone's feathers.

If you went to college, most likely you studied these temperaments. But I bet to this day you can't remember which one is which.

I have a confession to make. Neither can I. I studied all these temperaments in school (multiple times) and earned a doctorate degree in psychology, and I *still* can't remember which temperament label means what. I guess it's because the labels never did much for me. I'd never say to someone, "Oh, you're a sanguine." That sounds like they have a gangrenous foot or something else equally disgusting and slime green. And a choleric? It sounds like you've got a disease no one else would want to catch. (Mmm, are you sure a shot will take care of that?) And who wants to call someone "melancholy"? I love words, but *melancholy* is just not a nice word. I'd rather call someone a Communist pinko than tell them they're "melancholy." And phlegmatic? Use your imagination. Isn't that the mucus your neighbor's cat yaks up on your Berber carpet?

So instead I prefer to look at the personality types a different way. I'm a dog lover, for what it's worth. So since I'm the author of this book, guess what? We're going to talk about dogs . . . and they might just resemble you if you look closely.

> *I have a confession to make. I studied all these temperaments in school (multiple times) and earned a doctorate degree in psychology, and I still can't remember which temperament label means what.*

Yorkie All the Way!

Yorkies are sure cute as the dickens, aren't they? My sister-in-law Linda has trained her Yorkie to get her car keys out of her purse and bring them to her when she's ready to head out the door. Yorkies will be the first to greet your arrival, yapping wildly all the while. They're the life of the party, always ready for the next event. They have to be in on the action and can't stand being left out of it. In fact, their bodies quiver with excitement, and their ears perk up, as if they're asking, "Hey, what's next? And can I come?"

They don't know a stranger. They'll rush right on up to anyone and engage them in barking conversation as if they're the best of buddies and have been all along. They're Mr. and Miss Personality Plus, and what's more, they know it. They could get away with murder. They could sell ice cubes to Eskimos . . . or get you to take them outside for *another* walk, just because they see something interesting out the window and can't stand not checking it out. They're so charming and personable that they often get what they want, when they want it. And they're used to life going their way.

Yorkies are often called the "popular" ones (that's why they're called the "popular sanguine")—the social bunch, the kind you like to have show up at

Yorkies are the life of the party, always ready for the next event.

every party. Their motto is "Let's do it the fun way," and it's fun to watch them do it! Their needs are mostly social—that is, they want to be noticed, appreciated, affirmed, accepted, even adored.

Yorkies aren't difficult to identify. Search for the person who can talk about anything at any time in any situation, listen for the loudest person in the group, or watch for the person with the biggest smile. Yorkies are usually most comfortable in a crowd, or at least in a small group. They have a bubbly personality, an almost naive optimism, a strong sense of humor, and the innate ability to tell good stories. Most of all, they enjoy people and social interaction. They tend to be animated and playful, spontaneous and optimistic, funny and lively. They do great in the sales field, since they can motivate just about anyone to buy anything with their native charm.

But Yorkies also have weaknesses. They are so disorganized that they spend half their life looking for their car keys and the other half apologizing for missed appointments. They can't remember your name (but will be very offended if you forget theirs), have a tendency to exaggerate, and aren't particularly serious. Their "What? Me, worry?" attitude means they are more than willing to let others do the work, and their eternal optimism makes them prime targets for being deceived.

What gets Yorkies down? Boredom is a big one. They don't have much tolerance for that. Rejection is another. They live for approval and honestly can't believe that someone doesn't find them just *adorable*. Yorkies are practically allergic to budgeting either their time or their money—they get there when they get there, and if they want something, they'll probably buy it regardless of how much debt they carry. That new car on the showroom floor? It's theirs in five minutes or less.

If you want to make a Yorkie like you, it's pretty easy. Show an active interest in her, laugh at her jokes, and point out her positive characteristics. Do these things and you'll have a friend for life. Treat her well and she'll inspire, motivate, and entertain others—just don't expect her to follow through or pay attention to detail.

If you want to ruin a Yorkie's day, don't laugh at his jokes. Instead, criticize him or say something like, "Not everyone thinks you're cute." You'll see his face fall past China.

When under stress, Yorkies tend to leave the scene, go shopping, or find someone who approves of them. If they can't do that, they'll blame others for their stress or create some excuse for why they didn't get the job done, however lame.

> *When under stress, Yorkies tend to leave the scene, go shopping, or find someone who approves of them.*

I have a particular affinity for Yorkies. They're my favorite, in fact. Just my saying that should clue you in that I am, of course, a Yorkie myself. How does this play itself out? Let me show you.

When Sande and I were first married, money was really tight in the Leman household. One day I was walking through a shopping mall on my way to buy socks and underwear and got a glimpse of something in a jewelry-store window. The item stopped me short. It was so amazing that I did a double take, walked backward, and practically twisted my neck off just to get a second look.

Shazam! I thought. There, under the high intensity of a showpiece lamp, sparkled the most amazing timepiece I had ever seen.

It was incredible. Calling this thing a *watch* would be a massive understatement. It was practically the key to contentment, at least in my opinion. Its 48 diamonds around the face screamed, "I belong to someone important!"

Immediately I started talking to myself. *I've never seen a watch like that in my entire life.*

The clerk (she sure wasn't dumb as mud like me) saw her mark and quickly walked up, asking me if I'd like to hold it.

"Is that legal?" I asked.

She laughed. "Here, let's put it on you."

"Gosh, that's heavy," I said. "Is it gold?"

"Absolutely. It's 24 karat."

Before I could ask, "How much?" she said, "And it's on sale."

Shazam! It's on sale! Regularly $4,995, it was now going for a mere $3,800. Without thinking that the watch represented over four months of income, I whipped out my American Express card and took the watch home.

It may shock some of you when I mention that initially I had no remorse. On the contrary, at the stoplights I couldn't stop stroking my ear with my left hand, letting everyone see just how important I was—the watch proved it! Light jumped off that sucker like crickets off summertime grass.

About a mile from home, however, reality hit. My wife, Mrs. Uppington (see if you can figure out which personality type she is), would be waiting for me.

It happened the second I walked in the door. Sande took one look at my arm and said, "You bought that?"

"Yeah. Isn't it great?"

"That's the tackiest watch I've ever seen! How much did it cost?"

"It was sort of expensive, but I like it," I said, defending my purchase.

Are you getting the Yorkie personality? Back then I knew we didn't have anywhere near $3,800 to spend on a watch, especially when I could have purchased a workable one for 1 percent (or less) of that amount. But it didn't make me feel guilty to whip out the credit card. I saw something, I wanted it, and I bought it.

That's the Yorkie way: do something spontaneous, jump in with both feet, and ask questions later.

Three days later the dumb $4,000 watch stopped working! I was more than a little put out. You pay $3,800 for a watch, you expect it to last more than 72 hours, right? I went back to the store, but the lady who sold it wasn't there.

> *I saw something, I wanted it, and I bought it. That's the Yorkie way.*

"Hey," I told the new guy behind the counter, "my watch stopped, and it's only three days old!"

"Let me take a look at it," he said. "Oh, I see the problem."

"What's that?"

"You didn't wind it."

"You mean I have to wind this stupid watch?"

"Yes, sir."

A daily task—even one as small as winding a watch—is often more than a Yorkie can handle.

Today I still have the watch and wear it everywhere I go. (And yes, I did learn how to wind it.) Ask me to show it to you if you come to one of my seminars. Though I now agree with Sande that it's a bit gaudy, it serves as my reminder about how easy it is to get hung up on things. Someone like Mrs. Uppington would save the watch (of course, a very different kind of watch!) for very special occasions. Dr. Leman the Yorkie wears it all the time, and it shows. It's a diamond shy by now, with a few nicks.

I've learned as I've grown older that flashy isn't always good. Sande has helped me in that respect, but I still carry marks of being a Yorkie. I can't tell you how many times I've bought a used car without even starting it. If it looked right, it was mine. That's the Yorkie way.

If you're a Yorkie, you love the limelight. You're affectionate, make friends easily, and enjoy social activities. You're imaginative, creative, vivacious, lighthearted, and generous. You wear your emotions on your sleeve but are quick to forgive and forget. You love to promote new ideas on the job, so you're a natural at selling anything. But you may have problems with follow-through on tasks—doing anything new can be exciting, but rote tasks can quickly become dull, and you'll tend to lose interest if that activity is no longer engaging and fun. You may also struggle with being chronically late and tend to be forgetful.

Sitting in a toll collection booth on an interstate would be as close to putting a Yorkie in h-e-double-hockey-sticks as you can get.

Are You a Yorkie?

Pros

- popular, social
- want to be noticed, appreciated, adored
- humorous
- tell good stories
- animated, bubbly personality
- act spontaneous
- naive optimism

Cons

- disorganized
- let others do the work
- get bored easily
- can't budget time or money

- little attention to detail
- can't handle criticism
- if they see something, they buy it

There's a Reason a Great Dane Is Great

Put a Yorkie next to a Great Dane, and you'll see why a Great Dane is considered great. Everyone looks up to the Great Dane . . . literally. In fact, the first thing you say when you see a Great Dane is, "Oh my goodness! Look at that dog!" Great Danes capture people's attention. They're the leader of the pack in many ways. They have a certain presence and stature in the dog kingdom. They're the boss of their territory (and they act like it too). It's not often that other dogs even attempt to mess with them (and then those other dogs are really sorry they even made the attempt). One growl from that big beast and the littler dog will scuttle off, yelping, to go hide somewhere. And who could blame him? I wouldn't want to see a beast the size of a Great Dane galloping after me down an alleyway, that's for sure.

How My Life Changed

My brother and I can't get along. We were never able to even as kids. He's two years younger—and the family screwup. It all started when he got caught smoking a joint behind the neighborhood liquor store when he was 13. Ten years later, he's floating from job to job (which drives my parents crazy). I've always been an engineer and very goal-oriented. I've been at the same firm for three years.

I never took Jack seriously when he used to spout off, "Yeah, Mr. Perfect—that's my brother," when he was ticked off. But maybe that's really how he feels. After I heard you talk on the radio about how we become who we are, I called him last night for the first time in a year, just to see how he was doing. I don't know if he'll call back (we've ignored each other since last Christmas), but I know it's the right thing to do . . . and a step in the right direction.

Joe, Colorado

Great Danes (the "powerful cholerics") eat, sleep, and drink power and control. Whereas Yorkies say, "Let's do it the fun way," the Great Dane's mantra is, "Let's do it *my* way." Their favorite emotional menu is obedience (toward them, of course), appreciation for accomplishments, and respect for their ability. If you serve these dishes to a Great Dane on a daily basis, you'll have a strong ally. If you withhold them, you'll have a fierce adversary.

> *The first thing you say when you see a Great Dane is, "Oh my goodness! Look at that dog!"*

Great Danes come in handy when you need someone to take charge and make snappy (usually correct) judgments. Their self-confidence is high, and never once in their life have they feared hurting other people's feelings, so they tend to be decisive, firm, and commanding. You couldn't ask for a better military commander or football coach. They are adventurous, persuasive, strong willed, competitive, outspoken, daring, confident, and independent.

On the negative side, Great Danes can become a bit bossy, domineering, insensitive, and impatient. They expect immediate and enthusiastic compliance and can take it personally if their judgment is even questioned. While they don't appear to have any fears, if you scratch the surface a few inches, you'll soon discover they have a strong fear of losing control. Even the thought of mutiny could make them break out in a drenching sweat. Missing out on a promotion (or worse, being fired from a job), facing a serious illness, raising a rebellious child—these are the nightmare scenarios for control-oriented Great Danes.

Great Danes tend to be unsympathetic, unaffectionate, headstrong, proud, intolerant, short tempered, and overly dedicated to work. They get along best with submissive and supportive people pleasers who see things their way and who, when asked to jump, quickly respond, "How high?" If you really want to get on a Great Dane's good side, let them get the credit for something you've done. Cooperate with their suggestions and work hard to make them look good.

The reverse will soon make a Great Dane a bitter enemy. Steal their limelight, act like a rebellious troublemaker, question their judgment, sidestep their authority, or act independently, and just watch the steam come out of their ears!

Great Danes keep the world moving and improving. They are right most of the time and can accomplish more in ten years than most Yorkies will get done in a lifetime. They'd do even better if they could learn to delegate more and became a little more patient, but

The Great Dane's mantra is, "Let's do it my way."

true Great Danes will have to learn how to be more sensitive and less controlling—those certainly won't come naturally.

If you're a Great Dane, you'll instinctively respond to stress by becoming even more controlling. You'll put in even more hours at work, convinced you can solve any problem with just a little more effort. Your tolerance level in business is such that you'll shed few tears getting rid of a troublesome employee. You're a doer. You have a lot of ambition, energy, and passion, and you try to instill it in others (whether those others want it or not). You're an overachiever, so you think everyone else ought to be one too. Often you can't find anyone to do a task right, so you do it yourself. You have supreme self-confidence, like being in control, and are comfortable making quick decisions. But if you're not careful, you can dominate people of other temperaments.

Are You a Great Dane?

Pros

- take charge
- make snappy (usually correct) judgments

- high self-confidence
- daring, adventurous
- competitive
- persuasive, strong-willed, outspoken
- independent

Cons

- have to be in control ("my way or the highway") and expect others to immediately comply
- need to be obeyed
- need to be appreciated and respected
- insensitive (hurt others' feelings often) and impatient
- bossy and domineering
- fear loss of control
- unsympathetic, unaffectionate
- headstrong, proud, intolerant, short tempered
- overly dedicated to work

The Standard Poodle—A Cut above the Rest

When Sande and I were first married, we didn't have two nickels to rub together. But we had a puppy that we adored. One day Sande saw a sign at a nearby park about a puppy show. So we, being young and dumber than mud, thought, *Hey, our puppy is cute. Why not enter him in the show?* Off we went to the park to stand in a very long line of dogs and humans. When we finally reached the front of the line, a lady, pen poised, asked in a rather uppity manner, "What breed is your dog?"

Sande and I smiled at each other. "Uh, we really don't know. A mongrel, I guess. But he sure is cute, isn't he?" Sande said.

The lady pulled herself up into true aristocratic fashion and said huffily, "Well, I'll have you know this is for AKC [American Kennel Club] registered puppies *only*."

We were smart enough to get the message. "Well, fine," I said. "Enjoy your show. We're leaving." I tugged at my startled wife's elbow and off we went, our cute mongrel trailing after us.

The lady was such a Standard Poodle personality that I was surprised she didn't lift her leg on us. . . . But then, I guess that would be contrary to her gender, now wouldn't it?

I always think of Standard Poodles as a cut above the rest of us. They walk so stately. They have a certain gait to how they move too—almost as if they ought to be carrying a fine silk parasol in their paw. Their little kennels are air-conditioned, carpeted, and littered with little blue ribbons won at shows. They're classy and intimidating. They certainly wouldn't be caught keeping company with a mongrel. Standard Poodles are certainly not my kind of dog (so I guess that tells you something about me too).

So how does the Standard Poodle relate to a human being? Let me tell you a story.

I'm not very savvy when it comes to putting together anything with tools. So you can imagine my dismay when, after purchasing an "easy to assemble" dollhouse for one of our girls, about 1,385,432 parts fell out of the box. Sande's eyes went wide—she knows well that any more than five parts and I'm out of my league—and she said what I was thinking: "Better pay Roger a visit."

Roger is a perfect Standard Poodle. Whereas Yorkie says, "Let's do it the fun way," and Great Dane says, "Let's do it my way," Standard Poodle says, "Let's do it the right way."

> *Whereas Yorkie says, "Let's do it the fun way," and Great Dane says, "Let's do it my way," Standard Poodle says, "Let's do it the right way."*

I can't tell you how many times Roger stopped me when I was just about to do something and said, "Now, if we really want to do this right . . ."

Standard Poodle (also known as "perfect melancholies") put a lot of emotional energy into getting something done correctly. They have a strong emotional attachment to stability, and their need to get something right often translates into a need for space, silence, and sensitivity. While Great Danes get things done, Standard Poodles think about how it *should* be done. They're the philosophers among us who enjoy deep analysis, live by high standards and ideals, are skilled at setting long-range goals, and tend to be very organized. In addition to being highly analytical, Standard Poodles are usually respectful, sensitive, good planners, orderly, faithful, cultured, idealistic, thoughtful, and loyal— not a bad combination.

> *Standard Poodles are usually respectful, sensitive, good planners, orderly, faithful, cultured, idealistic, thoughtful, and loyal—not a bad combination. Their weaknesses? Think anal-retentive!*

Their weaknesses? Think anal-retentive! That's right—they spend too much time on preparation and worrying about messing things up. Their near obsession with details and the process means they can become easily depressed, weighed down by negatives, and suspicious of others.

If their high standards aren't met—or, just as hurtful, no one seems to care about them—it's hard for a Standard Poodle to even get out of bed. They may have nightmares about making a mistake and take it personally and deeply if they believe they are forced to compromise their standards or lower their ideals. They are insecure to begin with and tend to be rather unforgiving and resentful. Furthermore, their highly analytical nature makes them hard to please, pessimistic, negative, moody, and skeptical.

They are often loners. They are suspicious and, when crossed, can become out-and-out revengeful.

Standard Poodles love to hang out with the serious crowd. They look for people who enjoy deep discussions and have little patience for clown personalities. If someone is considered an intellectual lightweight or is disorganized, superficial, or even just plain old unpredictable, Standard Poodles run in the other direction—or marry them. (Yes, you read right.) They're famous for choosing a popular Yorkie spouse, hoping to piggyback on the Yorkie's social skills, then turning around and immediately trying to place their Yorkie on a disciplined schedule.

Fat chance!

If you're a Standard Poodle, you are marked by good manners and obvious attention to detail, including in your grooming. You're often a perfectionist, very particular about what you want and how you want it. That's why you're often dissatisfied with your own work and are always pointing out to yourself what could and should be improved. You're highly creative and very sensitive, and you pay a price for that. You are kind and considerate of others but hard on yourself. You can easily become overwhelmed and depressed by the sad or tragic things of life. Standard Poodles are often loners, choosing to stay alone and reflect rather than join a group.

Are You a Standard Poodle?

Pros

- do things "the right way"
- highly analytical
- live by high standards and ideals
- skilled at setting long-range goals
- very organized, orderly

- respectful of others, sensitive, thoughtful
- faithful, loyal
- love deep discussions

Cons

- anal-retentive (things have to be done correctly)
- need stability
- need silence, space, and sensitivity
- fear being forced to compromise their standards or lower their ideals
- insecure
- unforgiving, resentful
- pessimistic, brooding

The Irish Setter—Loyal as the Day Is Long

When I was a child, I had an English Setter named Prince. The dog was the most loyal companion in the world. Prince would walk me to school in the morning and be waiting in the same spot when I got out of school in the afternoon. That dog would sit there all day long waiting for me!

I was a creative child (now there's an understatement—some called me a little brat). There's even a photo in the Leman family photo album of Prince wearing my underwear (inverted, so his tail came out the fly) and a T-shirt (with his legs sticking out the two armholes), complete with a cigarette in his mouth. Now why would an eight-year-old do that to his dog? I have no idea.

But Prince? He never batted an eye. I can imagine what that dog was thinking: *If my master wants to make a fool of himself, I'm game. After all, he does flip me a Milk-Bone dog biscuit every once in a while . . . if he's not eating it himself.*

How My Life Changed

Bette, my co-worker, has driven me crazy from day 1. Anal is her middle name. If you suggest that she do anything different from the norm, she scowls and says, "Well, that wouldn't be right." I do the same projects, but I sometimes like variety in the way we do them or I get bored.

When you talked to our business group about why people are the way they are, I couldn't help but think about Bette. Understanding why she's the way she is and why I'm the way I am has made it easier to put up with her in the last two weeks. I've realized that her need to control everything is probably because she's insecure and scared of making a mistake, and that helps me not to take her crabbiness personally.

Bette hasn't changed (maybe someday I'll have the guts to explain to her why she is the way she is, ya think?), but the office is sure a lot less tense—at least for me—because I've learned how to work with her without setting her off.

And hey, who needs more stress at work anyway?

Angie, North Carolina

P.S. Think you could maybe come to our data office and speak to all of us sometime? If you do, I'll make sure Bette's invited!

And Prince would be right. I did eat Milk-Bone dog biscuits for a while there. (But only the Milk-Bone brand would do. Nothing else tasted right . . . even if I did it to be a show-off.) I tried to quit when I got married.

When I think of Irish Setters, I think of great family dogs. They're patient; they get along well with kids. If you have a three-year-old who likes to pull a dog's ears, an Irish Setter is the dog least likely to snap at the youngster for doing that. An Irish Setter is loyal to the core—and incredibly tolerant. They're balanced, loyal, and unswerving. They don't ask for much in life, and they enjoy pleasing others. They just want a Milk-Bone dog biscuit thrown their way every once in a while.

But they also won't set the world on fire. A bomb could go off next to them and their response might be, "Did you hear something?" Sometimes it's hard to get Irish Setters to respond, because they're so . . . calm. They don't like anything to rock the boat.

"Can't we all just get along?" That's the song of an Irish Setter (also known as a "peaceful phlegmatic"), who suggests, "Let's do it the easy way."

Irish Setters avoid conflict like toddlers run from bedtime. They devote a generous portion of their life to keeping the peace and sidestepping conflicts, though they are usually pretty good at solving problems objectively. They tend to have a balanced and pleasing personality, as well as an even disposition (they're always "just fine"). They're wonderfully adaptable, patient, obliging, and friendly, not to mention good at listening (you couldn't have a better neighbor). They run on the submissive side and seem to have the gift of being contented. Irish Setters are usually tolerant and diplomatic and go out of their way to be inoffensive.

> *Irish Setters avoid conflict like toddlers run from bedtime. They devote a generous portion of their life to keeping the peace and sidestepping conflicts.*

Their weaknesses result from their quiet side: a lack of enthusiasm and energy, and sometimes a chronic inability to make a decision. They don't want to disappoint anyone. While they are a calming influence to those around them—Irish Setters never get too easily excited, even in the midst of crisis—it wouldn't hurt them to become a little more self-motivated and a little better at setting goals. Their indecisiveness can become irritating, and some take a decided bent toward being worriers. Their mumbling speech and sluggish approach to life can border on laziness and aimlessness.

If you're an Irish Setter, you're generally content and kind. As a calm, cool, and collected individual, you're not likely to make impulsive decisions. You're often popular because you're rarely offensive. You have a keen sense of propriety and seek to fit right in. You're consistent, relaxed, rational, curious, and observant. That means you're a good administrator and a wonderful diplomat. You probably also have many friends, because you are reliable and compassionate. You hang in there until the very end of any project. Loyalty is your middle name . . . even if it takes you a while to get the project done. But your shy personality can also sometimes make you come off as lazy or resistant to change.

Are You an Irish Setter?

Pros

- keep the peace (a calming influence)
- can solve problems objectively
- have a balanced, pleasing personality
- patient, obliging, friendly
- loyal, good at listening
- content, adaptable
- tolerant and diplomatic
- don't make impulsive decisions
- stick to the end of a project (even if it takes a while to complete it)

Cons

- avoid conflict
- lack of enthusiasm and energy
- sometimes unable to make decisions because they don't want to disappoint anyone
- need self-motivation
- indecisive regarding setting goals
- sluggish approach to life (seen as lazy, aimless)

Have Wallpaper, Will Murder

Can personality typing explain *how* you became the person you are? No, but it's a good start because it describes you now, as you've become.

One of the most dramatic examples I've ever witnessed regarding the different personality types took place nearly four decades ago when my wife agreed to wallpaper my mom's kitchen. Two of my dad's friends showed up, both of whom happened to be retired colonels in the Air Force. One of them was obviously a Standard Poodle, the other a Great Dane. Being military men, they decided to take action and help my wife with the wallpapering. I have to admit, the Yorkie in me laughed and thought, *This could get fun.*

You have to understand, I married Martha Stewart's clone. If Martha ever took a vacation, Sande could step right into her place and probably increase Martha's television ratings to boot. The last thing Sande needed while wallpapering that kitchen was advice—but she was about to get plenty.

As suggestion followed suggestion, I could see Sande's temperature begin to rise. The melancholic colonel wanted this job done right. The Great Dane was adamant it be done his way, and it took the two men all of ten seconds to start raising their voices at each other.

"Now, Sande," the Standard Poodle said, "make sure you get that plumb line straight. Otherwise the entire job will be messed up."

"You sound like you know what you're talking about," I said. "Have you wallpapered much before?"

"He couldn't wallpaper a doghouse," the Great Dane cut in. "He hasn't papered a square inch!"

"Neither have you!" the Standard Poodle said in his defense.

This was too rich—neither of them had any experience wallpapering, yet both felt that Sande couldn't possibly do the job without their help.

Not even close to being deterred, the Standard Poodle weighed in with his preferred method. "The best way to do this is to put a weight on the bottom of your string there," he said. "Once the string is taut, you have your plumb line."

"Could you be any more dense?" the Great Dane said. "If she just leaves the line there, it'll move every time she touches it! She should chalk the line and snap it against the wall, then she won't have to worry about working around it."

I'm not sure how many plumb lines Sande has prepared—I'm guessing more than a dozen, not one of which took her more than five minutes. But thanks to these two guys, it took Sande a good hour and a half just to get a plumb line on the wall.

Everything became a battle between doing it "the right way" and doing it "my way." Both colonels had very strong opinions about where Sande should start to hang the paper. Both were even more forceful about how to cut a corner, how to paper over switches, and the best way to line up the paper against the ceiling. And when Sande reached an air-conditioning duct . . . my goodness, you would have thought the future of democracy was on the line by the way these men argued their cases.

> **Lies You Tell Yourself**
>
> It's gotta be *my way* or the highway.
> There's only *one way* to do things.
> There's only one way to do things *right*.

I couldn't help but chuckle when my mother, the classic Irish Setter, entered the scene. She was clearly uncomfortable with all the arguing, and as an Irish Setter, she was sure it was all her fault—after all, it was her kitchen that everyone was arguing over—so she went back to her old standby. In my mother's worldview, if there was a problem, you baked your way out of it.

"Can I get you gentlemen some cookies and coffee?" she offered.

She might just as well have landed on the beaches of Normandy during D-day and offered tea and biscuits. They looked at her like she was from another planet. *Cookies? Coffee?* they seemed to be thinking. *Are you crazy? We have a war going on here!*

Frankly, my mom should have stayed out of the kitchen. When she stayed, Mr. Standard Poodle and Colonel Great Dane enlisted her in the war.

> *She might just as well have landed on the beaches of Normandy during D-day and offered tea and biscuits. They looked at her like she was from another planet.* Cookies? Coffee? *they seemed to be thinking.* Are you crazy? We have a war going on here!

"What do you think of this corner, May?" Colonel Great Dane asked.

"It looks fine," Mom said.

"Fine?" Mr. Standard Poodle nearly shouted. "You think this is *fine*? Look at this bulge here. See? See the problem?"

"Oh yeah," Mom said, totally unsuspecting, "you're right."

"Of course he's not right," Colonel Great Dane cut in. He then spent five minutes making his case.

"Yes, yes, I see that now," Mom said, only to be accosted again by Mr. Standard Poodle.

When Sande started to book the paper (rolling it, putting it in a tub of water, letting it soak, then unfolding it to put it on the wall), I just about died laughing. Booking is a complicated process that needs to be done rather quickly. Sande is competent, but she's not a perfectionist. She just wanted to get the paper up on the wall, whereas the two colonels had their own agendas and were trying to direct her every move. This slowed Sande down and made the job that much more difficult.

I have to confess, the Yorkie in me couldn't stop from egging on the two colonels just a little bit. "You know, Ken, you ought to listen to him more," I said once. "He sounds like he knows what he's doing." Of course, I knew this would make Ken, the Standard

Poodle, furious and he'd plead his case all the more, but a Yorkie's role is to make things fun.

If you were in this situation, what role would you play? Would you be like me, goading people on and trying to have a good time? Would you be the Standard Poodle, concerned with the correct way to hang the wallpaper? Would you be the powerful Great Dane, who wants it done your way? Or would you be like my mom, trying to keep the peace as people go to war?

Whenever you're trying to keep the personalities straight, remember this story—Mr. Standard Poodle was determined to get things done *right*; Mr. Great Dane was just as determined to get things done *his* way; my mom, Mrs. Irish Setter, was insistent that everyone just get along; and I, Mr. Yorkie, wanted to have a really good time.

Eventually the inevitable happened—the two colonels stopped just short of coming to blows, and one of them stomped out of the house in a huff. Sande breathed a well-deserved sigh of relief until Mr. Standard Poodle broke in with the words, "Now that he's gone, we can really get this done right!"

I think you've got the picture by now.

"This all makes great sense, Leman," some of you might be saying. "But what if I don't fit any one particular mold?"

There's Just One You

As you read through the four personality types, you may have been thinking, *This sounds like me, but that one sounds a little like me too.* And now you're confused. Just which personality type are you?

The fact is, only a very rare person is 100 percent Yorkie, 100 percent Great Dane, 100 percent Standard Poodle, or 100 percent Irish Setter. Most of us are unique blends, and that uniqueness comes from our personalities as filtered through the experiences that shape us.

Your personality could very well encompass a couple of these dog breeds. For example, at work, you could be a Standard Poodle, a cut above the rest. But then you go home and you're a Yorkie who can't find your shoes without help. (Does that sound a little like your younger brother, who took nine years to get through college—then became a top architect at his firm two years later?)

Which characteristics of the personalities do you see in yourself? What unique blend of personality types might you have?

No one personality type is "better" than the other. They're just different. And different is what makes the world go round—in exasperating, funny, and memorable ways.

But why is it that, within a family living in the same household, there are so many different personality types? Shouldn't personality be at least partly stamped in our genes?

And why is it that Yorkies are most often babies of the family? Great Danes are often firstborn children in their family? Standard Poodles are often only children? And Irish Setters are most often middleborn children?

We'll discuss those questions—and more—in the next chapter.

What to Do on Monday

1. Decide you want to make a change.
2. Identity your personality type.
   - Yorkie
   - Great Dane
   - Standard Poodle
   - Irish Setter
3. Make a list of the personality traits you'd like to change.

Tuesday

Maybe You Do Belong in the Zoo!

> When you entered your family, you changed your entire family
> dynamic—much more than you think.

Sometimes my spontaneous side can get me in trouble. Take, for
instance, the day I said on a national TV interview, "As the baby,
I think it's strange that my wife, a firstborn, thinks things ought to
be written down—like checks. I'm content to let the bank tell me
what I have every month rather than go through all that trouble
to find a missing dime."

The host stopped me. "Wait a minute. You called yourself a
baby and your wife a firstborn. What do you mean, 'baby'?"

"Well," I said, warming up to my favorite topic, "I'm the youngest in my family."

"You know, you *do* remind me of my little brother," the host
said.

By her expression, I could tell her remark wasn't completely
complimentary.

I could also see that this conversation was going to take a sharp left-hand turn. It always does whenever birth order is mentioned. So, wanting to have a little fun (a lastborn or "baby" trait, by the way), I eyed the host's two sheets of interview questions, meticulously typed. I could see "Question #1," "Question #2," etc. Clearly she had built a ten-foot-high wall against any smidgen of spontaneity that might somehow sneak into her interview. There was no doubt in my mind now; I knew I was dealing with a firstborn.

> *"You know, you do remind me of my little brother," the host said. By her expression, I could tell her remark wasn't completely complimentary.*

This oughta be fun, I said to myself. Then I leaned over, took the notes out of her hands, crumpled them up, and threw them over my left shoulder.

"You don't need those notes," I told her. "Let's just talk to each other."

The host was horrified. Her hands flew to her face, and she looked as if she'd just seen a ghost. Then suddenly seemed to remember she was on live TV!

The production people lost it. They started howling behind the camera. It was evident they'd never seen the host put in this position before, and boy, were they enjoying it.

"Now you *really* remind me of my little brother," she said.

The firstborns watching that interview were probably thinking, *That little brat! He needs a good spanking!*

The lastborns? They were giving each other high fives and generally celebrating the start to a fun and different-from-the-norm interview.

The host reminded me of my oldest (and only) sister, Sally. Sally can't believe I can get up in front of ten thousand people and talk for an hour without using a single note card. She's even more dumbfounded that I can be given the topic just an hour or so before I get up to talk. When Sally speaks, she wants to rehearse her talk 42 times over a period of several months, and even after that she brings ten pages of notes with yellow highlights throughout. Spontaneity is not my sister's middle name.

After my host got over her shock, we had a wonderful talk. I'm convinced it was much better than the one we would have had if she'd stuck to her notes. True to my prediction, the host was a firstborn, like Sally. But I give her a lot of credit. The host even relaxed enough during the show to laugh (and hopefully forgive me for my spontaneity).

I love talking about birth order. I've studied it for years. It's a great icebreaker and a delightful form of entertainment.

But what do personality and birth order have to do with each other? Is our personality stamped on our genes?

If that were true—that you were simply born a certain personality type because of your genetic code—doesn't it seem odd to you that families aren't usually made up of just one type of personality (for instance, all Standard Poodles or all Yorkies)? Just imagine what the household would be like if they were! Of course, if an Irish Setter married a Great Dane, you might expect a mixture of the two, but how can you account for the fact that a large family will have all four personality types—and a host of blends—represented?

It's true that you are a product of the environment you grew up in. Your genes do create certain parameters and determine a lot about who you are and who you will become. But you are also greatly shaped by your experiences—the expressions you saw on your parents and siblings' faces when you were young, the words they said, and how they acted toward you.

For example, let's say you were just learning to walk and decided to give it a go by yourself . . . and you fell on your diapered bottom. How did your mom respond? Did she come running, frantic to help you? Did she laugh and say, "Uh, good try. Want to try it again?" Or did she simply ignore you because you weren't crying or bleeding and she had other things to do?

How your mom responded has a lot to do with your perspective of yourself (more on that on Wednesday). And these experiences have everything to do with birth order—your place and role in the family.

Lies You Tell Yourself

I can't change. I was born this way. (It's all in my genes.)
I'm just like my _____.
I can't help it. I'm only a product of my environment.

After years of studying birth order, I believe that a Yorkie *becomes* a Yorkie because she realizes the sibling above her is anything but a Yorkie (and she's driven, like I was, to gain attention in another direction). The firstborn is a Great Dane because his parents raised him in such a way that he takes on Great Dane (firstborn) tendencies. In short, children intuitively know what situation they are born into—and they learn to act accordingly to find their own place and role in the family.

So personality types describe who you are, but birth order helps to explain why you've become that way.[1]

Personality types describe who you are, but birth order helps to explain why you've become that way.

The theory behind birth order is simply this: the order in which you were born into your family shapes your personality in indelible ways. Firstborns generally share common characteristics, as do lastborns and middleborns. Birth order also takes into account that children react to the siblings above them, usually going in the opposite direction.

I believe that if you were to clone two women with the exact same DNA, then place one of them as the baby of the family with three older brothers, and place the other one as the oldest with three younger brothers, those two women would have markedly different personalities. They would still share some common characteristics, but the influence of birth order would largely prevail.

The oldest sister, more likely than not, would be a great nurturer of men, while the younger sister would be a better friend to men—she'd understand them better and might even be more of a tomboy than a mother. The women's intelligence would be the same, but how they used that intelligence and how they related to others would be remarkably different.

Your family of origin—and your role in that family—has everything to do with who you are now. And if you understand who you are now, as well as why you are the way you are, you can become that new you . . . the person you long to be.

Who's Who in Birth Order

Alfred Adler, the pioneer of birth order theory, says most of us fall into four basic categories: lastborn, middleborn, firstborn, and only.

The "Special" Entitled Ones: Lastborns/Babies

A friend of mine was talking to his eight-year-old daughter, the lastborn in his family, about a pack of Pez candy and a dispenser in a box of Cheerios. The middleborn son wanted the candy, the oldest daughter wanted the dispenser, and the youngest daughter wanted both.

"Why should I give you both the candy and the dispenser, while your brother and sister get nothing?" Dad asked his eight-year-old.

"Because I'm the youngest," she said.

Made plenty of sense to her!

Lastborns grow up with a tremendous, unflagging sense of entitlement. You usually don't have to convince lastborns that they are special—they already know it and will remind you of it every ten minutes should you momentarily forget. Because they are often coddled and babied—not just by Mom and Dad but also often by older siblings—lastborns usually grow up to be "people persons." Since everyone in the family is older than they are, they have learned the art of persuasion and occasionally even manipulation. They can charm you, are usually engaging, and are often blatant show-offs. An overwhelming number of comedians are lastborns.

> *Lastborns grow up with a tremendous, unflagging sense of entitlement. You usually don't have to convince lastborns that they are special—they already know it and will remind you of it every ten minutes should you momentarily forget.*

Some years ago, when I was doing a TV show on birth order, the producers told me they usually warmed up the audience with a comedian. But that time they took my suggestion to have the audience seat themselves according to their birth order. I assured them the results would be a humorous kickoff for the show.

After the host introduced me and the subject, she mentioned they had divided the audience according to birth order. Then she said, "Where are you only children?"

There was a smattering of polite applause.

"Firstborns?"

Again a polite applause.

"Middleborns?"

A little quieter applause.

"Lastborns?"

You would have thought this group had just won the Super Bowl! They shouted, jumped up and down, and waved their hands like they were trying to flag down a plane on a deserted island. And all that in response to a simple question!

Lastborns frequently give away their birth order just by their names. If you meet a 25-year-old Robbie, you're probably meeting a lastborn. A firstborn would have insisted on being called

"Robert" or "Rob" before he hit the job market after college. If you're introduced to an adult woman who goes by the name Krissy, Suzy, or Missy, you can bet you're talking to a baby.

A lastborn's favorite phrase might be, "I wonder what would happen if . . ." When you get the wedding photos back and see that one of the six-year-old crumb crunchers pulled his shirttail out of his fly, therefore spoiling the portrait, two to one says he's a lastborn. When everyone else throws rice as the happy couple races down the sidewalk, the lastborn thinks, *What would happen if I threw gravel instead?* (I actually pulled this stunt myself once, and my dad showed me exactly what would happen. It wasn't fun. And his discipline held me back from following through the next time I asked myself, *What would happen if I threw rice pudding?*)

> *A lastborn's favorite phrase might be, "I wonder what would happen if . . ."*

As the performers of the family, lastborns tend to take far more risks than their conservative older siblings, but they are also less industrious, cherishing the idea of "play now, pay later."

One exception: some lastborns can become very intense if they have a case of "I'll show them." Because they're often told that they're too young or too small or too dumb, lastborns can become very ambitious to prove others wrong. But along the way, they still love being pampered and spoiled and rarely lose their affection for the spotlight.

This desire to be the center of everyone's attention can manifest itself in many ways. Maybe the child will become the class clown. Maybe she'll become the weak, slow one the family always has to wait for whenever they take walks. Maybe he'll become the "messie" or the rebel. But all these different behaviors have one end in mind: making adults notice the baby.

Vocationally, lastborns are best suited for people-oriented jobs. Some babies could sell encyclopedias to illiterate families

How My Life Changed

I have 12-year-old twins. Anna can do anything she decides to do. She always gets her homework done on time, helps me around the house, and even packs her own and her brother's lunch (usually with the four food groups represented) in the morning.

Jason is my dragger. He drags everywhere. He forgets his homework at school, he's never around to do his chores (his sister always ends up doing them), and if it were up to him to make his lunch, he'd pack a box of Pop-Tarts and a soda and call it done. He's just about impossible to motivate.

When a friend gave me *The Birth Order Book*, pow—the light went on. And I finally got it. Ever since they were small, I've treated Anna like a firstborn and Jason like a baby. Talk about a self-fulfilling prophecy—they're it. Once I figured out what was going on, I talked with my sister (I'm a single mom), and we brainstormed some ways I could hold Jason more accountable to get things done and take the pressure off Anna for being the kid who has to do everything.

Old habits die hard. (I'm talking about myself here.) But yesterday Jason took the trash out of his room without being asked. (Hey, he still doesn't remember to take the trash out on trash day, but we're working on that.) One step at a time, huh?

Coletta, Tennessee

and make a pretty good living at it. I made a killing one summer selling magazine subscriptions, becoming the company's most successful salesman ever. That's because I learned to schmooze my way into a house to make my pitch. If I could make them laugh—and usually I could—more often than not they'd buy a magazine subscription.

Comfortable around people, lastborns are frequently extroverts, energized by the presence of other people and good in relationships. They're affectionate, uncomplicated, and generally cheerful (as long as you give them their daily diet of attention). They make great friends and companions.

Their weaknesses include an attention span of about five seconds. (I ought to know.) Lastborns hate to be bored almost as much as they hate to be rejected. If it's not fun, they want to do something else. They can be a bit self-centered and optimistic almost to a fault, which can get them into a lot of trouble. Babies have the tendency to rationalize, as in, "I know I don't have the money to pay for this today, but if I put it on a credit card, I'm sure I'll have the money next week."

To firstborns, lastborns may seem undisciplined and gullible. In the wrong personality type, the tendency toward attention seeking can become full-blown self-centeredness. Lastborns sometimes play the role of the rebellious child—temperamental and moody, spoiled and impatient. They frequently don't have time for unnecessary distractions like balancing a checkbook, putting their car keys someplace where they can find them, or picking up their room.

Lastborns hate to be bored almost as much as they hate to be rejected.

Though I've described lastborns as the life of the party, they can also go from laughing and joking to crying and being moody in a matter of seconds. Researchers aren't sure why this is, but I have my own theory: the baby of the family can be coddled one minute and berated the next. Though they are often treated as special by the parents, they are also frequently reminded by their older siblings that they are the runt, the weakling, or the stupid one. This can create an almost Jekyll-and-Hyde type of personality—happy and gracious one minute, sulking and depressed the next.

Quick Traits of Lastborns

- social, outgoing, have never met a stranger
- uncomplicated, spontaneous, humorous
- high on people skills
- see life as a party
- likely to get away with murder—and the least likely to be punished (they're too young and cute)
- wear a lot of hand-me-downs
- get picked on by their siblings
- keep their nickname

The Middlemen: Middleborns

I'm a proud supporter of the University of Arizona athletic program and have had the privilege of getting to know many of the coaches. Former head basketball coach Lute Olson provided me with an interesting insight into his 1997 championship team. Two of the top eight players were only children, five were firstborns, and just one was a middle child—Mike Bibby, a star point guard who now plays in the NBA. Lute told me that Mike was one of the most coachable players he'd ever had. As a middleborn, Mike didn't have the ego that the other players did. The point guard's job is to be the middleman, the guy who keeps everything together, and Mike, as a middleborn, played that role perfectly.

Middles usually take on the temperament of an Irish Setter. They like peace at all costs. Middles are the negotiators, the mediators, and the compromisers. Looked at cynically, they might also be considered the brownnosers, because they don't like confrontation. Middleborns want everyone to get along, and they tend to have a strong fear of being the one who gets blamed.

Middleborns want everyone to get along, and they tend to have a strong fear of being the one who gets blamed.

Middleborns are the hardest to define because a middle can go in any number of directions. Most often, that direction is the complete opposite of the child just above them in the family. For example, if the firstborn is a star athlete, the middle might become a scholar. If the firstborn is a gifted musician, the middle might spend her time racing motorcycles. What's the middleborn doing? Trying to carve out her own place in the world, which means diverting as far as possible from the firstborn's path.

Occasionally, the middleborn may think he can outdo his older brother or sister—the way Donald Trump and former presidents

Richard Nixon and George Bush Sr. did—and more than one middle has been known to follow this path with gusto. But if the middleborn doesn't think he can surpass the firstborn's legacy, he'll usually react by trying to create his own.

Gender takes on even more significance with middles. Middleborn boys who come from families in which all the children are boys tend to take on classic middleborn characteristics. But middle boys who have all female siblings often take on some firstborn characteristics because they are the firstborn male (the same is true for a middle female with all male siblings).

> *If the middleborn doesn't think he can surpass the firstborn's legacy, he'll usually react by trying to create his own.*

The classic middleborn is usually a good team player and is reliable, steady, and loyal. There are exceptions, depending on age gaps. Sometimes a middleborn will be a scrappy, ambitious climber just aching to pull down a firstborn, but that's not the norm.

How My Life Changed

A couple months ago, I was asked to head up a community event. I said yes, but then I got really uncomfortable and didn't know why. I'd done that kind of work before as part of a committee for the last four years. *So what's the problem?* I kept asking myself. My sisters (one's older and one's younger) do that kind of stuff all the time.

Well, I pulled off the event, but it was a mess. I tried to make everyone happy (and that never makes anyone happy). I'll never do that again.

Two weeks after the event, you spoke at a mother's tea at my church and I found out just how much of a classic middle child I am. The next time I get asked to be the head of an event, I'm going to say no. But I'm going to tell them I'd be happy to work on anything they ask me to do. Team player—that's me. Leader—no.

Thanks for setting me straight.

Jenny, Ohio

Middles aren't as comfortable making decisions as firstborns are. They have a higher degree of doubt than firstborns and consequently tend to be less gifted at solving problems (though they're great as mediators or when solving disputes). They roll with the punches and are amiable, down-to-earth, and great at listening. They can be unselfish to a fault and very loyal. They're the nice, polite, laid-back, and usually nondescript type of people. They don't stand out in a crowd and don't make waves, but they are very pleasant to be around.

On the negative side, middleborns may have a difficult time setting boundaries. They may try to please everyone and consequently frustrate everyone in the process. When something goes wrong, they will sometimes take the blame, even when they are not at fault.

Here's the middle's dilemma: Firstborn Frank gets all the respect. He's the oldest, the smartest, and the biggest. Lastborn Linda gets all the affection. She's the cutest, the smallest, and the one in need of most attention. Middleborn Mike gets squeezed out. He doesn't get the respect of the firstborn or the attention of the lastborn. In fact, what he most often gets is the blame. He can't out-argue Frank, and Linda gets excused because she's so little, so guess who has the finger pointing at him? And if Middleborn Mike ever gets so bold as to actually hit the little princess, he won't be able to sit down for a week.

Middleborns make excellent marriage partners. In fact, they represent the most faithful of all birth orders.

While middles defy easy stereotyping, in general they tend to be more secretive than their other siblings. Their frequent history of getting blamed leads them to play their cards close to the vest, so to speak, and to think that others have it in for them. (Richard Nixon was a middle child—enough said!)

Because they've had to forge their own way, middles are usually mentally tough and independent minded. They haven't been spoiled like the lastborn, and since they were often ignored, they learned early on that they have to make their own way. You won't see too many middles who hate the thought of moving out of their parents' house—they usually can't wait to get out on their own.

Middleborns make excellent marriage partners. In fact, they represent the most faithful of all birth orders. They may not be as fun as the lastborns or provide quite as well as the firstborns, but they tend to be very loyal, eager to please, and accommodating. They're sort of like a universal donor at the blood bank, because they fit in with everything and everyone.

Unfortunately, while one middle can be good, two middles married to each other can be a disaster. In my counseling practice, I once talked to a couple of middle children who'd gotten married but, in two years of marriage, had yet to consummate their vows. I got a clue what the trouble was when the mother of the groom was the one who made the appointment! She knew *someone* had to step in and do something. When I talked to this couple, I felt like I was talking to two kids on the playground—one was saying, "You start it," and the other was saying, "No, you start it." With both of them being middles, it just never got started!

As middles, both of them feared conflict even more than they wanted to enjoy sexual intimacy. If you're not a middle, you probably just can't understand that. If you are a middle, you're nodding. You get it.

The Prince/Princess in Waiting: Firstborns

You already know the firstborn. You may have voted for him to become president. Or maybe you work for her at a Fortune 500

> **Quick Traits of Middleborns**
> - go the opposite path of the child above them in the family
> - walk to the beat of a different drummer
> - competitive, loyal, big on friendships
> - live in an anonymous haziness (the safest place to be)
> - can get away with occasional laziness and indifference (they're not noticed as much)
> - aren't pushed as hard or expected to accomplish as much as the child above them
> - good negotiators who try to keep the peace

company. Perhaps you watched him fly into space as an astronaut or you've read one of her bestselling books. All of these occupations are overwhelmingly populated with firstborn adults.

Firstborns are pretty easy to spot. Every hair is in place, their clothes are immaculate, and their shoes are shined. Their cars are vacuumed, and they're the ones who buy Palm Pilots and Day-Timers (and actually use them). You can count on them to be prompt, and their easygoing confidence is obvious by the way they shake your hand and look directly into your eyes.

> *Firstborns are pretty easy to spot. Every hair is in place, their clothes are immaculate, and they're the ones who buy Palm Pilots and Day-Timers (and actually use them).*

I call firstborn children "adults in kids' bodies." They are known for being capable, hard driving, perfectionistic, exacting, exhaustingly logical (just get into an argument with one, and you'll know exactly what I mean), scholarly, and organized. I know of one firstborn pro golfer who is known for hanging his shirts in his closet according to the order in which he'll wear them. I'm not joking. When a reporter asked him if this was really true, the golfer seemed surprised. "How else would I organize them?" he asked. It didn't even occur to him that a vast number of people never even think to organize their closets!

Though firstborns like to be in charge, this desire for control can produce different results. Some firstborns will be the type A bosses who rule through power. Others will be the compliant nurturers who take care of the world as nurses or teachers. If the firstborn is raised by a critical parent (more on this in Wednesday's chapter), the child may learn that the way to get along is to be cooperative and easy to work with. Rather than taking charge, these firstborns are best suited for middle-management roles—they will get a task done and do it correctly, but they don't want to take the lead and won't rock the boat.

72

How My Life Changed

I'm a firstborn. No surprise. I'm driven, I'm organized, and I get more done than anyone else in my division at work. I don't have much free time. When I was married, my wife used to complain that I never made it home in time for dinner. She didn't understand how important my projects at work were.

Life was going well—I even got the manager job I'd been aiming for—until my wife asked me for a divorce. Then everything fell apart. I felt lost. I was in a bookstore one day and saw your book *Born to Win*. I read it straight through while I drank three Starbucks. You pegged me. I never realized that all the firstborn qualities that made me succeed at work were working against me at home and made my wife feel unloved and unappreciated.

I guess you can't go back, but you can go forward. Now I'm making a conscious effort at work to include other people in my decisions instead of just running the show (which is a lot easier sometimes!). When I go with friends for dinner, I don't answer work calls. And I started to play racquetball again . . . for fun.

I wish I would have seen your book two years ago. But then, I was too busy to be in a bookstore.

Timothy, New Jersey

My wife, Sande, is a compliant firstborn. She was once served a piece of salmon so raw it could have started swimming upstream if you put it in a river, but she refused to send it back—until her lastborn husband, who doesn't have a compliant bone in his body, did the job for her.

Firstborns rarely fall far from the tree. As the parents go, so do the firstborns—in action, in thought, in all of life.

Many firstborns are very meticulous. Any profession that requires exactitude sounds good to them. Airline pilots, accountants, astronauts, and other such occupations all tend to be filled by oldest children. If you need to get something done,

Quick Traits of Firstborns

- reliable and conscientious
- list makers
- black-and-white thinkers
- keen sense of right and wrong
- believe there is a right way to do things
- natural leaders
- achievement oriented

73

if you want to start a business, if you're looking for someone to bring organization to chaos, you'll be served best by a firstborn. She'll get the job done, and done right.

The One and Only: Lonely Onlies

I call only children "super firsts." Take the best and worst qualities of a firstborn and magnify them two or three times, and you'll create the recipe for an only. Onlies are leaders, and they tend to be super perfectionists. Everything is black and white, meaning, "Do it my way or the wrong way." Because of this, they tend to be critical and a little selfish. They can sometimes run over people and may have little regard for others' emotions.

> *Take the best and worst qualities of a firstborn and magnify them two or three times, and you'll create the recipe for an only.*

A typical only is a list maker, is a scholar, and thrives on logic. He tends to be very neat (but even the few "messies" know exactly where to find something amid their piles). Onlies are the mega-movers of the world—task oriented, extremely well organized, very conscientious, and ultimately dependable. They love facts, ideas, and details and feel very comfortable with responsibility.

Only children may be introverted. Though they enjoy one-on-one interactions, they have little patience for group small talk at social events. They are often unforgiving and very demanding. They hate to admit they're wrong and usually don't accept criticism well.

The special situation of onlies can create two different kinds of people. The first seethes underneath the surface. He was raised on a tightly structured, highly disciplined plan and was expected to be and to act grown up from the time he was five years old, having lived around adults and socialized primarily with adults.

He can be very cool and calm on the surface, but underneath he's very resentful because he was cheated out of his childhood.

The other situation is the "crown jewel of the universe" syndrome. When both parents pour their love, energy, adulation, and financial resources into the only—treating her as the center of their universe, always making her feel super special—the only can take on lastborn traits.

Whatever the case, only children are well represented among those who have accomplished much: US presidents Gerald Ford and Franklin D. Roosevelt (the only man to be elected four times); actors William Shatner, Brooke Shields, and Robin Williams; magician extraordinaire David Copperfield; influential evangelical leader Dr. James Dobson;

> *Onlies are the mega-movers of the world— task oriented, extremely well organized, very conscientious, and ultimately dependable.*

How My Life Changed

I'm a bristler. I admit it. It's really easy to tick me off—especially if you say something you haven't thought through very well. My husband is a spontaneous sort who likes to just "announce" things. About once a week, we'd get into a slam-dunk fuss. . . . Okay, call it what it is: a fight. I'd tell him he needed to consider me and think through his decisions; he'd tell me I needed to lighten up—and that not everything has to have a five-point plan. Then one of us would spend the night on the couch.

Then I heard you talk about birth order on an early morning radio talk show as I drove to the grocery store. I'm an only child, and my parents were in their forties when I was born. They were so happy to finally have a kid that I was the center of their world. I always got my way. Then enter Frank (my husband), who didn't always see things the same way.

That night I made Frank his favorite dinner and apologized to him for acting like such a brat. (I was.) I really love the guy and want our marriage to work. Tonight we're going to go get that book you talked about, *The Birth Order Book*, and we're going to read a chapter together every night.

Tricia, Michigan

**Quick Traits
of Only Children**

They share all the traits of
firstborns:

- reliable and conscientious
- list makers
- black-and-white thinkers
- keen sense of right and
  wrong
- believe there is a right
  way to do things
- natural leaders
- achievement oriented

And more:

- take all the traits of firstborns a step further
- love books
- act mature beyond their
  years (are little adults by
  age seven or eight)
- work independently
- can't understand why
  kids in other families fight

and football greats Roger Staubach and Joe Montana, legendary quarterbacks in the National Football League. And don't forget Leonardo da Vinci, the Duchess of Windsor, Charles Lindbergh, Indira Gandhi, and Isaac Newton, who have all made their mark on history.

This is the one birth order that occasionally fools me during my seminars. I might peg someone as a baby of the family, but they'll proudly correct me: "No, I'm an only child!" When they say that, I can tell them a lot about their childhood and how they were probably quite spoiled growing up. In virtually all cases, they'll sheepishly admit that, yes, the house was centered around them—the little prince or princess.

But What about the Exceptions?

Some of you are saying, "I'm not sure I swallow what you say about birth order, Dr. Leman. I mean, my brother's a lastborn, but he certainly doesn't act like it. And my firstborn sister? She doesn't have the traits of a firstborn at all."

Ah, maybe birth order isn't quite as simple as who is born first, second, third, etc., in the family. There's more to it.

Our daughter Lauren—who was born when Sande was 47 and I was 49—is a good example of an exception. We should have known something was up the first time we laid eyes on her. Sande and I both have brown eyes; late-in-life Lauren popped out with green eyes and a CEO personality: "All right, world, I've arrived. Time to get everything in order."

You'd think that this youngest of five would end up being the family mascot, spoiled rotten and great at putting people in her service.

Nothing could be further from the truth.

You see, there's a large gap between Lauren and her next oldest sister, Hannah—over five years—making Lauren very much like an only child. And this only child has at least six parents, since our other four children love to tell her what to do. At nine years old (a particularly colorful year of memories with Lauren), she was noted for saying things such as, "Well, I'll take that as a no," with her legs crossed demurely like a refined young socialite. When I'd see her doing that, I'd think, *Where did she come from?* It sure wasn't from a guy who likes wearing the same pair of shorts, rumpled T-shirt, and baseball hat three days in a row.

Birth order isn't quite as simple as who is born first, second, third, etc., in the family. There's more to it.

At that time, Lauren also had a pet hamster named Sugar Foot. Pity the poor fool who visited our house and mentioned Lauren's "gerbil."

"It's not a *gerbil*," she'd say forcefully. "It's a *hamster*." (Ah, do you see the only child character traits popping up?)

As a family, we had a habit of fleeing the hot oven known as Tucson near the beginning of June, finding refuge at a lake house near Jamestown, New York. When we prepared to make our annual pilgrimage that year, Lauren found a neighbor boy in Tucson who was willing to watch little Sugar Foot.

Like a typical only child would do, Lauren got out a big piece of colored construction paper and wrote out "Instructions for Sugar Foot." The paper contained no fewer than 12 very specific rules, covering Sugar Foot's physical and emotional well-being, including, "Stroke Sugar Foot's back softly, but be careful that you never spook him."

Reading over this very exhaustive list, I was struck by how thoroughly Lauren had done her job. Having read the 12 rules, I knew exactly how Sugar Foot should be cared for.

Had I known nothing about this little girl, I would have assumed I was reading the work of an only child—yet Lauren is our fifth child. So what's going on?

A second example from Lauren.

I, the chubby psychologist from Tucson, have told parents numerous times in my books and seminars, "Don't major in the minors." But let's just say there was a time in the Leman household when it would have pleased me greatly if nine-year-old Lauren had consented to getting her hair cut. Lauren has nice thick hair, but it was way too long and unruly, and she was always playing with it because she was hot. (Keep in mind that we live in an area where coyotes start searching for lemonade in April.) Summer was coming up, so I thought it would be a great time for a shorter style.

I started with hints and suggestions: "Lauren, your hair is getting *so* long, sweetie."

No response.

"You know," I teased, "when you're sleeping tonight, I could get some scissors and save you some money by cutting off your hair. You wouldn't feel a thing."

"Oh, no, no, no!" she'd exclaim and protectively grab her hair.

Then one dark day, I even bribed Lauren. I promised her I'd take her to that cheese-breath rodent place if she'd just agree to get a more manageable hairstyle.

No such luck.

So you can imagine my surprise when I walked into my house a few months later and discovered that Lauren had gotten her hair cut—by her own choice. It looked wonderful, cut just below her ears and turned up at the ends.

I was beside myself with joy. "Lauren, I love your hair. It's absolutely adorable."

Lauren merely nodded as if it were no big deal. "I only let the lady cut my hair because she agreed that she'd cut it exactly as I wanted it done. I told her it could be short as long as we flipped it up like one of the Dixie Chicks."

Think about it: a nine-year-old kid went out of her way to tell me that the only reason her hair was cut short was because it was done exactly the way she wanted it to be done.

Only child, thy name is Lauren!

Except that Lauren is the lastborn of five. What's going on here?

Variables That Can Adjust Birth Order

Lauren is a prime example—still to this day—that a number of variables can adjust birth order.[2]

The numerical order of your birth (or entry into the family, if you're adopted) is significant and long lasting, but other factors contribute to who you are too.

Spacing

In Lauren's case, the spacing of the children in our family made a big difference.

Any gap of five years or more between siblings is significant. I know a young man whose two older siblings—both males—are eight and ten years older than him, and he has developed classic firstborn tendencies as a result. For many years, he met with an accountability group made up largely of middleborn guys . . . until they threw him out. His constant harping about doing things the right way and keeping everything on schedule and arguing over the most minor details was too grating to the laid-back middles.

Any gap of five years or more between siblings is significant.

Lauren can't really remember living with her three oldest siblings—they were all out of the house before she turned five—and there are more than five years between her and Hannah, so in many ways she has adopted some only-child tendencies.

Sibling Gender

A quiet, reserved firstborn female may have a very ambitious, firstborn-oriented little brother, particularly if there are other siblings who follow. Melanie, a firstborn daughter, is a compliant nurturer. She lives a very quiet, unambitious life and is happy at home. Her brother, Theo, is a hard-charging, ambitious little boy, driven to excel in everything he does—and he wants to do a lot: Boy Scouts, sports, you name it.

Being a firstborn male or firstborn female is significant, even if you are actually the third or fourth child in the family.

Physical, Mental, or Emotional Differences

If an older sibling becomes ill or disabled (as was the case in Richard Nixon's family), the younger child can pass the older and take on firstborn characteristics. Or the second, more naturally gifted child can end up overshadowing the older sibling, reversing the roles—and thus reversing the stereotypical effect of birth order.

The Blender Effect

Sibling deaths, adoptions, divorce, and remarriage—all of these occurrences can shuffle traditional birth order characteristics. It can be earth-shattering for a 10-year-old firstborn to lose a parent, then get a "replacement" parent along with a 12-year-old sibling who unseats him as the firstborn. And the parents wonder why they have World War III in their home.

The Birth Order and Personality of Your Parents

There's one more factor that affects how you respond to birth order, and that's the birth order into which your parents were born. A firstborn mom will, on average, run her home much differently than a lastborn mom. The lastborn mom will tend to be less strict about her children's eating and sleeping schedules (lunch may well be served at 2:00 p.m.), while the firstborn mom will usually have a more orderly approach to child rearing. A middleborn dad will often value peace above all else, while a firstborn dad may push all his children to achieve. Each one of these parenting styles will affect you to a different degree. (More about this in the Wednesday chapter.)

> *The lastborn mom will tend to be less strict about her children's eating and sleeping schedules, while the firstborn mom will usually have a more orderly approach to child rearing.*

Perhaps the most devastating diverter of birth order is to have a critical parent. An unceasing barrage of antagonism will eventually wear down even the hardiest child, eroding the confidence of a firstborn or the "be happy" attitude of a lastborn. Criticism is like a personality virus; it can wipe out the strongest personality.

For example, perhaps you're a firstborn reading these pages, and you're described as a leader, a scholar, and a mover and shaker, yet you see yourself as anything but; you feel defeated, since you're great at starting things but lousy at finishing them; your expectations have sunk lower as the years have rolled by—if so, you could well be what I call a "defeated perfectionist." You're so full of potential and so talented, but you've been decimated by a flaw-picking parent (or worse yet, two flaw-picking parents) who *still* seemingly sabotage your every move. If this is your story, there's hope for you. Pick up my book *Why Your Best Is Good Enough.*[3]

> *Criticism is like a personality virus; it can wipe out the strongest personality.*

Birth Order Isn't an Exact Science

One summer two of our daughters, Hannah and Lauren, helped with a local program for three- to four-year-olds. I loved picking them up and hearing all the stories. Each day I was greeted with, "Dad, my legs are *so* sore from having those babies on my lap" (from Lauren), and "Dad, you wouldn't believe what little Chloe did today!" (from Hannah).

On the final day, several of the adult leaders came up to me and said, "I just want you to know what a joy it was to have Lauren and Hannah here to help out. They came in every day, knew exactly where to go, got their assignment, and then did it! On top of all that, when you put them together, you'd never know they were sisters by the way they get along so well."

All right, I know what you're thinking: *Hey, Leman, what's up? I thought kids who are next to each other in birth order are supposed to be night-and-day different! How come your two kids get along so well?*

Hannah and Lauren *are* very different in some respects, but they also get along extremely well. The age gap (over five years) between them removes a lot of the competition Sande and I witnessed among our three older children. Having had what amounts to almost two separate families, I also know that although certain birth orders carry specific traits, birth order isn't always easily defined.

One time a woman came up to me after a seminar and said, "Dr. Leman, I see a couple different birth orders at work in my personality."

"If you see a couple different birth orders, you might be a blend," I responded.

"What's that?"

"Well, let's take a look at your family."

"I'm the youngest, with an older sister and three older brothers," she said.

"You're from a large family—that's usually where you see the most blends. By the time you came along, you had veteran parents, which can also affect birth order tendencies, but I'm guessing that a number of traditional birth order elements are still part of your personality."

"Like what?"

"Well, since you're the youngest, and your older sister is so much older, I'm guessing that by the time you were a toddler, your older sister was sort of like a second mom," I said.

"Yeah, she really was—I wanted to be just like her. She was a librarian, and I always wanted to be a librarian."

"I'm also willing to bet that you were treated differently than your brothers."

"How so?" she asked.

"Did you ever hear your mom call you and your sister 'the girls'?"

"Not very often. Because of the age gap we didn't do all that much together."

"That's what I thought. You were seen as individuals. Now how many times were your three brothers referred to as 'the boys'?"

"All the time."

"They were a unit, weren't they? You've got the oldest, the middle, and little Schnooky. And I bet most of them follow traditional birth order patterns."

"They really do. My oldest brother does kind of act like the firstborn, and I can see my next oldest brother being the family peacemaker."

"Now, tell me, which brother did you have the most difficulty getting along with?" I asked.

"That's easy—my youngest brother."

"I'm not surprised, but why do you think that is, now that you've heard me talk about birth order?"

"Well, he was treated like the youngest in some ways, since he was the youngest boy, but . . ."

"But he didn't get the privileges of the lastborn once you came along?" I finished for her.

"That's right."

"Do you see how he might have resented that? You sort of usurped him as the baby. In a family of just three boys, he'd have your pride of place."

A little light blinked on behind her eyes. "Now I see. Yeah, he often told me that he resented me. Now I know why. I guess I still really am a product of my environment."

"The good news is, with three older brothers, you probably feel very comfortable around men."

"I do."

"Allow me to let you in on a little secret: men love it when women understand them as males. You've got a perfect background to have a very enjoyable marriage."

"That's encouraging!" she said.

> *If you've learned to become the product of your environment, you can unlearn the negative aspects and build on the positive ones.*

If you've learned to become the product of your environment, as this woman clearly did, you can unlearn the negative aspects and build on the positive ones. In the case of this woman, I wanted her to see why she and her youngest brother had so much conflict—but I also wanted her to begin thinking about how having brothers could prepare her for a happy and successful life.

How can you use your knowledge of your birth order to be who you want to be—and to accomplish what you want to accomplish? How can you capitalize on your strengths, overcome your weaknesses, and reach your full potential?

Make the Most of Who You Are!

If part of your personality is really working for you, let's build on that. But if one side of you is starting to wear more than just a little thin (at least from the perspective of others!), let's change that.

Elizabeth had an unusually compliant firstborn. This was the type of baby who slept through the night, who lay calm on the changing table while her diapers were being changed, and who practically thanked her mother for putting her down for her nap times.

When I saw her hold her second child, I couldn't resist telling her, "Do you realize what that little boy is going to be like?"

She looked at me like I was crazy. How could I know? This baby was less than six months old! "No, not really," she said.

"He's going to be Attila the Hun. You've already raised one saint, and that little sucker's gonna find out soon enough just what he has to do to get the same attention."

She was skeptical, assuming the compliance of her first child was due entirely to her and her husband's innate (and terrific) parenting skills. As it turned out, I was right. That boy grew up to be as different from his sister as rugby is from chess.

> *He was solely responsible for his parents' decision to have just two children—they didn't want to risk having another child like him.*

Fast-forward a number of years—the boy is now a teenager and in my counseling office after having gotten himself into one scrape after another. The parents think he's demon possessed. After all, they've already proven they could raise one angel, so where did this devil come from? He was solely responsible for his parents' decision to have just two children— they didn't want to risk having another child like him.

When I walked the young man through his family environment and the pressures he must have felt growing up with such a perfect, compliant sister, he was finally able to see, for the very first time, the force to which he had been reacting all his life.

"You wanted to be noticed," I explained. "That's natural. But you couldn't be noticed by doing what your sister had already done—being inordinately cooperative and good. If you were going to get your parents' attention, you'd have to find an entirely different route—you'd have to cause trouble."

I could see him nodding. Knowing he was ready for the next question, I slipped in, "So tell me, is it working for you?"

"Is what working for me?"

"Is the rebel role giving you what you want? Do you like getting suspended from school, having lowlifes for friends, being on a first-name basis with the local cops, and having a future that, at best, puts you working the pumps at the local Texaco for the rest of your life?"

Look on the Bright Side!

Take an inventory of your positive traits. How can these qualities help you succeed?

"That's not what I want," he confessed, then quickly added, "but I don't want to be like my sister either."

"Of course you don't."

We then did a short survey of his strengths. Believe it or not, this guy was a leader. He didn't have any trouble getting kids to follow him. Since he was the firstborn son, that didn't surprise me. The problem was, he used his leadership in such a way that people got hurt and laws got broken.

"You can still be a leader," I said, "but now I want you to think first about where you want to take people. Do you want them to follow you to jail, or do you want to do something positive?"

Over the course of the next several weeks, we discussed and built on his other positive traits: people skills, creativity, and willingness to take risks (his firstborn sister didn't have a risk-taking bone in her body). We began to develop a composite of how these same qualities could help him succeed in a positive way.

Understanding the Family Den

If you were to visit me and we started talking about birth order, I'd ask you to create a picture of your "family den." I'd want to know about mama bear, papa bear, oldest child bear, baby bear, and so on.

Let's take Andrea, for example. She's number three of four kids—she's seven years younger than her older brother, six years younger than her older sister, and two years older than her younger sister.

Older brother: 39 years old

Older sister: 38 years old

Andrea: 32 years old

Younger sister: 30 years old

Pretend Andrea just walked into my counseling office. I begin by saying, "I want you to take a step back and look at the cubs that came out of your parents' den. Let's choose one word, an adjective, to describe each person's personality. What adjective would you use to describe your oldest sibling?"

"I guess I'd call him ambitious and a leader."

"I said *one* word."

"All right. A leader. But he really was ambitious. Today he's president of his own company."

"What about your big sister?"

"Oh, I don't know what's up with her. She's sort of the oddball maverick of the group. Cheryl has the least in common with anyone in our family. We're lucky if we hear from her at the holidays."

"Okay, we'll mark child number two down as the maverick who rebelled against the whole family. Just as a curiosity point, is she well organized?"

"Heavens, no! We called her Pig Pen."

"What about yourself?"

"That's what I don't understand. I read *The Birth Order Book* and pegged myself as acting like a firstborn, even though I'm not. In fact, my husband laughed at me last week because we had company coming over in an hour and he caught me cleaning the top of the refrigerator. 'Andrea,' he said, 'Marty is only five foot eight, and his wife is shorter than that! The only way they're going to see the top of that refrigerator is with a ladder.' But I just can't help myself. If I'm the thirdborn, how come I'm acting like a firstborn?"

"I'll come back to that, but for now let's move on to your youngest sister," I said. "Give me an adjective for her."

"She fits the mold, the classic princess who can do no wrong. I think she was my dad's favorite, although he never admitted it."

"What does she do today?"

"She's a stay-at-home mom, but she sells Mary Kay cosmetics on the side."

"A lastborn who's in sales? That's not too big of a shock. How does she do?"

"She's the best, which you can tell from five blocks away."

"What do you mean?"

"She has a bright pink Cadillac in the driveway," Andrea said. "Of course, they give other options nowadays, but Missy has always been a show-off."

"All right, we'll call Missy the princess. Now, back to you: why don't you understand yourself?"

"I'm so much like a firstborn, but I'm a thirdborn. That just doesn't make any sense to me."

"Let's look at the big picture. Your oldest brother was . . . what?"

"Really, really successful."

"And everyone looked up to him?"

"Yeah. Everyone went to him with their problems, including me. He's a really good brother."

"Can you see, though, that your older sister may have felt squeezed, like she couldn't compete with that older brother? And if life wasn't hard enough trying to compete with Mr. Superman, you come along and get everyone's attention. Now you're the mascot of the family. Everyone adores you. But at the same time, that six-year gap almost makes you the firstborn of the second family, doesn't it?"

"You know, it does. I guess I never thought of it that way, but I'm certainly Missy's big sister. Our other sister didn't want to have anything to do with her."

"Now the picture's a little clearer. Your older sister is taking on the role of the rebel. When you came along, someone had to step up to the plate and take on some responsibility—which you did. Then your youngest sister is born, and right above her is a feminine version of the Superman big brother. So what does she become?"

"Irresponsible with a capital I?" Andrea guessed.

"That's right, and do you understand why?"

Label Your Siblings

What one word would you use to describe each of your siblings? Here are a few to get you thinking.

- Scholar
- Athlete
- Troublemaker
- Rebel
- Mom's favorite
- Dad's favorite
- Pushy
- Bossy
- Leader
- Miss Goody Two-shoes
- Little Miss Perfect
- Bully
- Clean freak
- Geek
- Computer whiz
- Loner
- Saint (very religious)
- Business titan
- Control freak
- Substitute mom (or substitute dad)
- Adventurer
- Poet
- Activist
- Comedian

What does this word convey about your siblings' role in the family? Their birth order?

"Because I was so responsible; is that what you're saying?"

"That's exactly what I'm saying," I said. "That's why the very things that make you get uptight seem to her like a fun challenge; that's why she drives a pink car and you drive a black minivan."

It's only by working to gain a better understanding of how your siblings influenced your own role in life that you can more objectively evaluate the personality you've developed in response, as Andrea did. Then you can decide, as a mature adult, whether those traits are working for you.

So are they? If not, isn't it time to do something about them?

How to Make the Best of Your Birth Order

I'm going to say this loud and clear: none of the birth orders are better than any other, they're just different. If you're a tricycle person, there's nothing wrong with that. Just stay in the tricycle lane! Get out of the motorcycle lane, or else risk getting run over.

> *None of the birth orders are better than any other, they're just different.*

Every birth order personality has something to offer. Even rebels have their place. In a sense, Nelson Mandela and Moses were both rebels. They challenged the status quo and worked to make a positive change. We need people who make us laugh as well as meticulous people who can prepare our taxes. We need people to run for office and build successful companies, just as we need people who can resolve disputes and work through mediation. This world has a place for you, regardless of what title you think best fits your profile.

If you're a lastborn, getting an accountant's degree because that's what your older brother did probably isn't going to work for you. Those four walls will start to feel like a prison unless you can get out and have some social interaction. As a lastborn, you'll find that there are other occupations tailor-made for you.

If you're a middle child, ask yourself if you really want the pressures that come with being the top dog at work. Do you want to be the person whose decision will either run the company into the ground or finally make it financially profitable? Do you want to play the role of the bad guy who has to fire incompetent or lazy employees? If not, don't think that makes you less competent than a firstborn. It just means you need to find a different role to play at work.

If you're a firstborn, don't be surprised if lastborns steal attention away from you or if middles seem to enjoy long, relational discussions while you are left out of the loop. Relational small talk probably isn't your bag—you'd try to start solving that person's problems inside of five minutes. Relaxing is not a whole lot of fun to you.

Making Your Peace

Once you understand your birth order, other people may not seem as annoying to you. You no longer have to guess why your roommate is so messy, why your supervisor is so bossy, why your co-worker can't handle change, and why your neighbor always has to get his own way.

It also can smooth family relationships and bring reconciliation. For example, if you realize that your tendency is to go in the opposite direction of the sibling above you, it can clear the decks with your siblings, and you'll no longer have to ask, "Why can't I be more like my sister?" or "Why can't my brother be more like me?" And it should no longer be a mystery to you why a sibling took off in the direction she did. Based on birth order, that direction probably makes perfect sense.

If you grew up fighting with your siblings, understanding that your close proximity made you ideal candidates to go to war can take the "personal" out of the fight. Then you can look at the situations that caused your fights more objectively and begin re-building a new type of relationship.

I know what I'm talking about. My two oldest daughters were born less than two years apart. They never stopped competing with each other—and in some ways, they're probably still competing. My two youngest daughters have a big age gap, and they have been two of the most cooperative sisters I've ever seen. While I'd like to take some credit for this—and I do believe Sande and I have improved our parenting over the years—the truth is, a lot of their relationship has to do with birth order dynamics and the variables.

The same understanding can also help put your parents' actions in perspective. Most parents identify with the child of their own birth order. If Mom is the baby, she'll naturally feel closest to the baby. If Dad is a middle child, he'll look out for the middle child, knowing firsthand how easy it is for middles to get neglected.

> *If Mom is the baby, she'll naturally feel closest to the baby. If Dad is a middle child, he'll look out for the middle child, knowing firsthand how easy it is for middles to get neglected.*

When you replay your memories with birth order principles in mind, how does your thinking change? Perhaps you're a firstborn, and your lastborn dad seemed to have a soft spot for the baby of your family. But did that mean he didn't love you? No, it was just a naturally occurring phenomenon. Your dad was a baby of his family, and he's only human. His reacting the way he did—pampering and protecting the baby—said nothing about your own self-worth. But it said everything about your dad's own history. Life is too short to take this personally.

The irony here is that while parents identify with children of the same birth order, they also tend to butt heads with those children. A firstborn dad and a firstborn son likely will have some knock-down-drag-out scuffles. Hopefully fists will never fly, but boy, their strong wills and desire to control will create quite a few sparks. In the same way, two firstborn co-workers may continually duke it out verbally, and two lastborns in an office may have a hard time accomplishing anything (they're too busy swapping stories).

What does all this mean? Give yourself and others a heavy dose of grace. Break long-standing feuds. Reconcile with that difficult co-worker or sibling. Consider giving that parent a second chance. Don't take natural slights personally. Realize that everyone makes mistakes . . . and that includes you.

You'll never be perfect, but by understanding your personality, your birth order traits, and the variables that affect your birth order, you can

- identify your weaknesses and work on them;

- become familiar with your strengths and make them even stronger;

- understand your tendencies as a firstborn, middle, lastborn, or only, and bring a complementary circle of friends and people into your life that will help balance you out.

What to Do on Tuesday

1. Identify your birth order.
   - lastborn (baby)
   - middleborn
   - firstborn
   - only
2. Look at the traits of your birth order's personality. Which ones are like you? Not like you?
3. Look at the variables.
   - Spacing: Are there more than five years between you and the sibling above you?
   - Sibling gender: Are you the first of your gender in the family?
   - Physical, mental, or emotional differences.
   - The blender effect.
   - The birth order and personality of your parents.
4. Could you be a blend? For instance, you might be a middleborn, but due to the variables above, you've also assumed many of the roles and characteristics of a firstborn.

Bonus Section for the Curious
Who's Who?

Why are these famous people the way they are? It has everything to do with their birth order.

Guess Who?

Look back at the quick traits of lastborns or babies (page 67),
middleborns (page 71), firstborns (page 73), and onlies (page 76).
Then take your best guess at the birth order of these well-known
people. (See page 240 for the answers.[1])

Barack Obama	Steve Martin
Robert De Niro	Dwight Eisenhower
Hillary Clinton	Ellen DeGeneres
George Bush Sr.	Anthony Hopkins
Eddie Murphy	James Earl Jones
Martin Short	Bill Cosby
Laurence Fishburne	Whoopi Goldberg

Jay Leno

Tommy Lee Jones

Harrison Ford

Matthew Perry

Grover Cleveland

Stephen Colbert

Jennifer Aniston

Angelina Jolie

Brad Pitt

John F. Kennedy

Steve Carell

Jon Stewart

Billy Crystal

Chuck Norris

Sylvester Stallone

Danny DeVito

Drew Carey

Reese Witherspoon

Jim Carrey

Ben Affleck

Oprah Winfrey

Richard Nixon

Chevy Chase

Ronald Reagan

Donald Trump

Classic Examples of Birth Order

Ever wonder why Hollywood folks are the way they are?

Following are the real-life stories of famous people who are classic examples of each birth order. How did birth order play a role in who these people are and what they've accomplished? See if you can figure it out.

Hint: What you learn can help you find the "new you" too.

Oprah Winfrey

Firstborn Doing It Right

You may know that Oprah was nominated for an Academy Award for her work in *The Color Purple*. But did you know it was Oprah's first movie? Isn't that just like a firstborn? You take up acting, get nominated for an Academy Award, and then go find something else to do—like become the wealthiest black female entertainer of all time.

Oprah knows success. Her daytime show has been number one for years, and when she launched her own magazine, it went right to the top—the most successful magazine debut ever. Oprah also launched a series of all-day seminars entitled "Live Your Best Life." The 1,600 seats in Baltimore—at $185 a pop, mind you—sold out in 47 minutes.

Not everything she touches turns to gold (the movie *Beloved* didn't fare so well), but if you could buy stock in a person, you couldn't do much better than placing a large percentage of your IRA in Oprah, Inc.

> *Oprah was nominated for an Academy Award for her work in* The Color Purple. *But did you know it was Oprah's first movie? Isn't that just like a firstborn?*

I've met Oprah. In fact, I thoroughly embarrassed myself on her program. This was in the days before Oprah was OPRAH. She was generally well known but not a household name like she is today. During the first segment of the show, I kept referring to Oprah by her name, as I do with all hosts. I like to be friendly.

Imagine how embarrassed I was when the producer walked up to me during the first break and said, "You're doing a really great job, Dr. Leman, but her name is Oprah, not Ofrah."

Despite my mistake, Oprah must not have been too upset with me; she invited me back four times.

True to firstborn form, Oprah doesn't just want to entertain—she wants to make a difference. "I don't have any particular hopes or dreams for the future," she told *Good Housekeeping*. "I'm just a voice trying to help people rediscover their best selves." In an article she wrote herself, Oprah states, "I want my work, all my work—movies, books, television—to be a light in people's lives." To that end, in 1998 Oprah took her audience of over 20 million on a self-improvement exercise, calling her program "Change Your Life TV."

This theme has pervaded Oprah's work throughout her career. In a 2000 commencement address at Roosevelt University in Chicago, Oprah told the graduates, "There is a sacred calling on each of our lives that goes beyond this degree you're about to receive. There is a sacred contract that you made, that I made, with the Creator when we came into being. Not just the sperm and the egg meeting when we came into the essence of who we were created to be. You made a contract, you had a calling. And whether you know it or not, it is your job to find out what that calling is and get about the business of doing it."

Oprah's horrific childhood is well known. Though a firstborn, she had little privilege. She was born into a very poor family, was sexually abused and raped, and at age fourteen gave birth to a child who died. Given her poor start, Oprah's accomplishments are even more amazing.

Firstborns are often scholarly—or, at the very least, they usually have a few books on their bedside table. Oprah is a well-known friend of books. She describes her ideal weekend as gobbling up three books and staying in her pajamas. Oprah's Book Club almost single-handedly revitalized a flagging publishing industry, particularly for novels, practically guaranteeing the chosen books a place on the national bestseller list.

> *"There is a sacred calling on each of our lives. Whether you know it or not, it is your job to find out what that calling is and get about the business of doing it."*
> *—Oprah*

In fact, books had a big role in helping Oprah overcome her difficult start. She said, "For me, getting my library card was like getting American citizenship." As Ron Stodghill wrote in *Time*, Oprah used "the iron-willed protagonists she found in black literature to fire her dreams of rising beyond the back-breaking work that seemed the destiny of most of the black people she knew."

Like my firstborn wife, Oprah is a pleaser. She once regaled a Baltimore audience with stories about her "disease to please." Not all firstborns are pleasers, but a number of them are (particularly those who are women).[2] Oprah has talked about how this need to please used to hold her back until she reined it in: "Years ago, when I was running myself crazy trying to please everyone, I told Sidney Poitier it didn't matter how hard I worked, I couldn't seem to do enough to live up to other people's expectations, and he said, 'That's because you're carrying their dreams. What you have to do is find out what you expect of yourself and learn to live with that.' That really helped me a lot. I had to let go of other people's expectations and learn to live from the purest part of myself."

> "I had to let go of other people's expectations."
> —Oprah

Though a pleaser, Oprah still likes to be in control—another typical firstborn trait. She still signs all checks more than $1,000 for her business, Harpo Entertainment Group, and meticulously scrutinizes the smaller ones that others sign for her. She binds employees at all levels to strict, lifelong confidentiality agreements. And she guards her off-air ventures as fiercely. When Hearst (the publisher of O magazine) planned to co-position Oprah's first magazine issue with *Cosmopolitan* magazine by putting the two publications together in one special display, Oprah got on the phone and stopped them. "I am not going to be used to sell one of your other magazines," she said. "*Cosmo* is not who I am."

> Oprah is very loyal and expects 100 percent loyalty in return. If you want to get on her bad side, just violate her confidence—you're gone.

Though somewhat controlling, Oprah is extremely good to her staff. She likes to take them shopping, and from having been on her show, I know her assistants would do just about anything for her. Oprah is very loyal and expects 100 percent loyalty in return. If you want to get on her bad side, just violate her confidence—you're gone. In the book

Legends, Maya Angelou wrote a moving tribute to Oprah: "She was born poor and powerless in a land where power is money and money is adored. Born black in a land where might is white and white is adored. Born female in a land where decisions are masculine and masculinity controls. This burdensome luggage would seem to indicate that travel was unlikely, if not downright impossible. Yet among the hills of Mississippi, the small, plain black girl with the funny name decided that she would travel and that she would do so carrying her own baggage."

Perhaps without realizing it, Angelou goes on to mention that behind Oprah's startling success is her role as America's big sister: "She is everyone's large-hearted would-be sister, who goes where the fearful will not tread."

What a great label. Everything Oprah does, millions want to copy. We read the books she recommends. We listen to the guests she invites into her studio. And even when she does something crazy, like run a marathon, we follow. Maybe it's a coincidence that the year after Oprah ran her marathon in Washington DC, marathon attendance increased 15 to 20 percent, but Oprah's trainer, Bob Greene, doesn't believe that: "[Oprah] has a tremendous effect on people. . . . Over the years she's been willing to go public with her life and her struggles, and people identify with her." I think we're just eager to follow our big sister.

> *Behind Oprah's startling success is her role as America's big sister.*

Oprah has found her strength in reaching out to others. She has gladly accepted the role of America's big sister. Instead of letting herself be buried by bitterness, she has used her traits to help others—and it's come back to bless her. Oprah told a *Newsweek* reporter of one incident in which a man stopped her just to thank her for her impact: "I think it really is an amazing accomplishment that I grew up a little Negro child who felt so unloved and so isolated—the emotion I felt most as a child was loneliness—and now the exact

> *Oprah used that stinging sense of alienation to push her in a positive direction—one of changing the world.*

opposite has occurred for me in adulthood. Usually people just move through the future carrying the weight of their past. But for me, things have come absolutely full circle. I feel embraced by people's love. I think that is a tremendous gift."

Oprah used that stinging sense of alienation to push her in a positive direction—one of changing the world.[3]

Along with Oprah, other firstborn entertainers and actors include Harrison Ford, Matthew Perry, Jennifer Aniston, Angelina Jolie, Brad Pitt, Chuck Norris, Sylvester Stallone, Reese Witherspoon, and Ben Affleck. Bill Cosby, one of the greatest comedians of all time, is also a firstborn. Cosby, who holds a doctorate degree, is a perfectionist. He gave all of his children names beginning with "E"—to remind them to always seek excellence.

If You're a Firstborn . . .

You may never be the life of the party. You might rub some people the wrong way with your perfectionistic ways. But you can get a lot done, more than lastborns could ever dream about. You will have your own struggles to overcome—loneliness, perhaps, or a tendency to please others if you're a compliant firstborn—but if you'll face these obstacles head-on, there's little you can't do. You were born to succeed.[4]

Robert De Niro

The Only One

Actor, director, and producer Robert De Niro Jr., winner of two Academy Awards and a Golden Globe, is a classic only child.

Noted for his attention to fine details, he's gained a reputation for being one of the greatest and hardest-working actors of all time. He was ranked in *Empire* magazine's "The Top 100 Movie Stars of All Time" list in 1997 and voted as the best actor of all time at FilmFour.com in 2002. He was also inducted into the Italian-American Hall of Fame in 2002.

According to the Robert De Niro website, "Over the course of nearly forty years, Robert De Niro has established himself as one of the most respected and iconic screen actors in history. This is a position he's achieved both through the relentless perfectionism of his approach of his work, and the ferocity with which he protects his private life."[5] This perfectionism, drive, and intensity are all character traits of an only child. To all who've seen a De Niro film, there's no doubt he towers above all in his acting ability.

Robert De Niro was born in New York to two respected artists—Virginia Admiral, a painter, and Robert De Niro Sr., a painter and sculptor—who divorced when he was two years old. De Niro grew up in the Little Italy area of Manhattan with his mother, though his father (who had moved to Europe) visited regularly. De Niro was a shy boy who preferred reading over playmates (a trait of only children—books are their best friends). Many renowned painters, poets, and critics visited his home. (Again, another experience of only children—being surrounded by those older than you and perfectionistic or excellent at their craft.) Interestingly, when his father visited, he would take young De Niro to the movies. Afterward, De Niro would act out the movie he'd just seen, learning how to portray the characters. He first discovered his love for acting when he was 10 years old, and he played the Cowardly Lion in a school production of *The Wizard of Oz*. Seeing his acting ability, his mother enrolled him in New York's High School of Music and Art, but he dropped out to run briefly with a local street gang.

> *Perfectionism, drive, and intensity are all character traits of an only child.*

However, De Niro wasn't sidetracked for long (another trait of only children). By age 16, he was touring in a production of Chekhov's *The Bear*. At 17, after leaving the movies with a friend, he stated that he was going to be a film actor. Then he dropped out of his senior year of high school and went to acting school.

De Niro spent much of the 1960s working in theater and off-Broadway productions. His first "break" came when director Brian De Palma cast him in *The Wedding Party*, but that film wasn't released for six years. Then, in 1973, he met director Martin Scorsese (they had grown up in the same neighborhood but had never interacted as children) through the movie *Mean Streets*. He also played Bruce Pearson, a major league baseball catcher struck down by Hodgkin's disease, in *Bang the Drum Slowly*. To play Pearson's character, De Niro researched his part by tape-recording Southern voices.

This same attention to detail—delving deeply into the portrayal of the characters—is what has marked De Niro's career. For example, he worked as a cab driver for three months for *Taxi Driver*; learned how to play the saxophone for *New York, New York*; lived in Sicily for *The Godfather: Part II*; and learned to speak fluent Sicilian in order to portray the mafia world well. (His performance as young Don Vito Corleone in *The Godfather II* earned him his first Academy Award for best supporting actor—the first actor to ever win an Academy Award speaking only a foreign language! Now there's an only child for you.) For the movie *Raging Bull*, De Niro trained as a boxer with the street-tough fighter Jake LaMotta for an entire year before the film was produced. He also gained 60 pounds for that movie, showing the great lengths he would go to create an authentic character. The film *Goodfellas* solidified De Niro's fame with an exceptional performance.

In the late 1980s, he formed his own company—TriBeCa Films. "There's these guys," De Niro said, explaining why he started the company, "we call them suits. They have the power to okay a film. They're like your parents, going, 'We have the money.' But at the same time they say to us actors, 'We love you. We can't do without you.' You know, I've been around a long time. I've seen the suits run the asylum. I think I can do it as good or even better. Let me try it."[6] Did you catch that? "I can do it as good or even better." That's also a trait of an only child.

And he didn't stop with forming his own film company. He also co-owns several restaurants in New York and San Francisco. What he does in his private life, though, stays private. You rarely see a reference to Robert De Niro in the tabloids because he stays guarded about his personal life, and few details are known about him. When the press does comment on him, he seldom bothers to defend himself or give his side of the story. But every once in a while, there is a glimpse of his heart. At the 1981 Academy Awards, he wore a green ribbon on his lapel in remembrance of several African American children who were victims of a serial killer in Atlanta.

> *"You'll have time to rest when you're dead."*
> *—Robert De Niro*

Robert De Niro has shown himself to be an exceptional, focused individual who is respected by others and passionate about all he does. He drives himself toward whatever goal he's pursuing. As De Niro himself said, "You'll have time to rest when you're dead."[7]

What only children often lack, however, is the ability to cut back and enjoy a family. De Niro has been married twice—the first time, for twelve years to Diahnne Abbott. Then in 1997, nine years after their divorce, he married Grace Hightower, only to file for divorce two years later. However, to their credit (especially in Hollywood, where relationships continually change), the two somehow managed to smooth over the rough waters, since they renewed their wedding vows and are still together to this day.[8]

Other only children who are well known for their dramatic, and sometimes comedic, roles include Laurence Fishburne, Anthony Hopkins, James Earl Jones, Tommy Lee Jones, William Shatner, and Robin Williams.

If You're an Only Child . . .

Know that it's okay to set out to change the world. Your drive to succeed and achieve a rare state of excellence will inspire all of us. But do yourself a favor—let your hair down a little. Learn to enjoy life in the process. Find a loving man or woman who can make you laugh and lighten up now and then.

There are things in this world that need to be changed. But there are also things to be enjoyed. Don't sacrifice one for the other.

David Letterman

In the Middle and Fighting for Respect

David Letterman, a middle child (second of three), is in the same profession as Oprah Winfrey—both are part of the entertainment industry. But firstborns like Oprah Winfrey and Angelina Jolie will seek to change the world. Lastborns like Jay Leno and Julia Roberts will be universally loved for their work and their likable nature. And middleborns in Hollywood will, more often than not, be fighting for respect. That certainly has been the case with David Letterman.

> *Middleborns in Hollywood will, more often than not, be fighting for respect.*

The most vivid example of birth order taking center stage occurred in the early nineties, as Johnny Carson retired and Jay Leno was chosen to replace him as host of *The Tonight Show*. For years Letterman was seen as the prince in waiting, the comedian expected to get the biggest job in television on the longest-running show in history. He was clearly Johnny Carson's choice (Johnny is also a middleborn, by the way).

Interestingly enough, Jay Leno is a lastborn with classic lastborn tendencies. According to one journalist, "At one point in his life Jay thought he would be a funny insurance salesman." Jay developed his humor early on. He was mildly dyslexic and compensated by providing his friends and teachers with laughs. His fifth-grade teacher wrote out a report card that is typical for a lastborn: "If [Jay] used the effort toward his studies that he uses to be humorous, he'd be an A student. I hope he never loses his talent to make people chuckle."

In order to get the job on *The Tonight Show*, Jay worked the system. He was a great schmoozer, so he did special presentations for local NBC affiliates, gave lots of interviews to local papers, and did all the PR stuff to get his name out there. He also did crazy things like hiding in a closet to hear conversations about who was going to be chosen, and he admittedly went out of his way to politick and campaign for the coveted spot. Babies are born manipulators, and they love the thrill of the chase, so it's not a surprise to me that the lastborn won the game.

> *"I just like to think that if you work really hard and do a really nice show, people will like you. Ha."*
> —David Letterman

Middles tend not to even play, which Letterman himself admits. When told that Leno said, "I like the game," Letterman responded, "I didn't know there was a 'game' involved in this. Or I don't acknowledge it or I don't play it." One writer pointed out that Letterman was "too polite to grease his own ascension." Letterman explains, "I just like to think that if you work really hard and do a really nice show, people will like you. Ha. Ha. And then, 16 years later, you find out: not necessarily!"

Like most middles, Letterman tends to be pretty secretive, which doesn't match his profession all that well. When Bill Carter, who wrote a book on the Leno-Letterman battle to succeed Johnny Carson, appeared on Tom Snyder's talk show, Letterman called in, disguising his voice and taking on the persona of a trucker, rambling about any number of issues. He later told another reporter that his sole purpose for the call, which seemingly went on forever, was to keep the book writer from talking about him as long as possible. "I just didn't want to hear them talking about that [stuff]," he told writer and friend Bill Zehme.

Letterman might seem eccentric to others, but I see a middleborn trying to make it in a lastborn's world. He even hired a worker to clear the corridors as he passes so no one can look at him or stop him to talk.

> *In spite of all his success, Letterman still can't see himself as successful.*

In spite of all his success, Letterman still can't see himself as successful. Once, he was on the deck of a spectacularly beautiful Malibu beach home, looking off into the Pacific Ocean, when he said wistfully, "I wish I could have something like this."

His host looked at him with astonishment. "Dave," he replied, "you *can.*" Zehme explains, "Luxury embarrasses him; he prefers to believe himself undeserving. That he reportedly earns . . . [millions of dollars] per year does not register at all. In his mind, he dwells but a heartbeat away from failure and ruin."

Though it might sound tough to say this, while Letterman has been very successful, I'm not surprised he's had a rough go of it. He's a middleborn doing a job tailor-made for a lastborn. His former producer, Robert "Morty" Morton, admitted as much: "[Dave is] basically the same guy up until show time. Then he assumes a different personality for that hour, but afterward he's right back again." While middles can rise above their birth order, they're still going to pay a price for stepping out onto unfamiliar, and certainly uncomfortable, ground.

James Wolcott, writing for the *New Yorker*, analyzes Leno and Letterman this way:

> On any given night, the difference between Letterman and Leno isn't one of talent or material but one of temperament. Leno . . .

is a Las Vegas vending machine of predictable jokes. Letterman is less containable. . . . Letterman has flared up over technical flubs and miscues that have dragged out the taping of his show, and has indulged in acts of self-loathing bordering on masochism, the most blatant example being the time he pummeled a life-size dummy of himself on the air, giving it repeated shots to the head. His neurosis has achieved classical dimensions. I happened to be reading Dr. Karen Horney's "The Neurotic Personality of Our Time" recently, and (except for the pages that reminded me of me) almost every chapter cried out, *Dave, Dave, Dave.*[9]

> *While middles can rise above their birth order, they're still going to pay a price for stepping out onto unfamiliar, and certainly uncomfortable, ground.*

Though Wolcott doesn't use this language, what he's essentially saying is that Leno is a typical lastborn, and Letterman is a fairly typical middleborn. He remarks, "It's questionable whether [Dave] can ever be happy on the air, given his irreconcilable desires to be the magnetic center and to be left . . . alone"[10]—classic middleborn behavior.

Letterman has done his best to remake his job, though, in the mold of a middle. He told one journalist, "Every day is a compromise." Just about every middle child will take on that attitude; I've never heard a lastborn say that. Another writer described Letterman as "America's great leveler."

> *"Every day is a compromise." Just about every middle child will take on that attitude.*

Also like many middles, Letterman seems to be pretty loyal. When the time came for him to shake things up and actually fire someone, he did it in classic middleborn style. "Because we'd never done it before, we took our time, and we ended up counseling these people, and it went on and on," he said. "And at the end of the day . . . we were just limp, we were exhausted, it was a horrifying situation."

It was also a situation you won't find many firstborns or lastborns getting into. In fact, Letterman can take this almost to an extreme. When a woman was arrested and prosecuted for stalking him in a rather scary fashion, the public prosecutor insisted that Letterman was never "vindictive. He wanted her to get help." A lastborn like me would have wanted a crazy person like that to be locked up (and have the key thrown away!).

A middleborn's loyalty inspires more loyalty. In spite of the fact that Leno took over Carson's old show, Johnny spent the next year making three appearances on Letterman's show without appearing on Leno's show once.

Take note of Letterman's expectations of failure, self-loathing, and discomfort with the spotlight. You'll see similarities in the lives of many middleborns. But David Letterman has used the best of his birth order to accomplish the most.[11]

Other middleborns who have used their birth order to a tremendous advantage are George Bush Sr., Dwight Eisenhower, Grover Cleveland, John F. Kennedy, Richard Nixon, and Donald Trump.

If You're a Middleborn . . .

Realize that you get a bad rap from everyone in your family. It would be easy to fall into the "poor me" trap—the squeezed-middle-child syndrome. Instead, remind yourself that middleborns end up as people like Donald Trump, Steve Forbes, and Bill Gates—all of whom have done rather well in life, wouldn't you say? Quite frankly, the fact that you never had Mom and Dad to yourself and that you negotiated and compromised for everything you got in life—not to mention the hand-me-downs you got from older brother or sister—have prepared you better than anyone else in the family to do life as it should be lived.

Jim Carrey

The Legendary Lastborn

Jim Carrey continues a long line of classic comedians stretching back through Jerry Lewis and Laurel and Hardy. Few actors of any kind can match his incredible run of hits, including *Ace Ventura: Pet Detective*; *Batman Forever*; *The Mask*; *The Truman Show*; *Liar, Liar*; and *Dumb and Dumber*. But did you know that this talented actor attended formal school only up through the ninth grade and that his growing-up years were far from easy?

James Eugene Carrey was born in a town just north of Toronto in Canada in 1962. He had three older siblings—Pat, John, and Rita. His mother, Kathleen, suffered from depression and was often sick with illnesses both real and imagined. Carrey went out of his way to entertain his mom—to help make her feel better—by doing impressions by her bedside of praying mantises and well-known TV stars. Percy, Carrey's father, was sharp-witted and highly amusing. He was formerly a sax player in a big band but had sold his sax and his dreams to take a job as an accountant. His father-in-law always referred to the mild-mannered Percy as "loser." (Carrey later modeled *The Mask*'s Stanley Ipkiss on his father.)

From the very beginning of his life, Carrey craved attention—from his family and from everyone else—and went out of his way to get it. He loved Christmastime, when visiting relatives increased his audiences. He was obsessed with TV shows, perfecting impressions of the stars (and also of his alcoholic grandfather), and putting on one-man shows in the basement of his home. In junior high, Carrey "performed" so much as the class clown that the teachers soon realized the only way to calm him down was to allow him a ten-minute slot at the end of each school day to entertain his classmates. (Mmm, this baby of the family can relate with loving the limelight. Now, if only *my* teachers would have been that smart when I was growing up. . . .)

By age 10 he'd already tried to publish a book of his poems and had mailed his résumé to the producers of *The Carol Burnett Show*. He wore his tap shoes to bed in case his parents needed cheering up.

Then, when Carrey was in ninth grade, his family was plunged into poverty when Percy lost his job and was forced to sell their house. The family moved to Scarborough, an industrial area on the edge of Toronto. In order to make ends meet, the whole family took jobs as security guards or janitors at the Titan Wheels factory. Carrey worked an eight-hour shift after school, scrubbing toilets, all the while determined to escape to a better life. His school grades suffered since classes were no longer a priority. Carrey felt more comfortable vandalizing the neighborhood with his brothers and performing for his bedridden mother than trying to compete at school for the grades he knew he couldn't earn.

> *Carrey craved attention—from his family and from everyone else—and went out of his way to get it.*

Eventually the Carrey family got fed up with factory life and quit. They soon became homeless, living for a while in the family Volkswagen van on a relative's lawn until they could move back into Scarborough.

About that time in his life, Carrey says, "My family kinda hit the skids. I was angry at the world for doing that to my father."[12]

When Carrey was 15, he made his debut at Yuk Yuk's comedy club, dressed in a yellow polyester suit with tails, which was made by his mother and similar to what he'd later wear for *The Mask*. The event was a disaster, but Carrey didn't give up. At 16, he dropped out of high school to start a career in stand-up comedy. Percy, who battled manic depression but was something of a comedian himself, helped Carrey write his first routines. Carrey wanted to be like his personal hero, Jimmy Stewart—an all-around nice guy but, unlike Percy, no pushover.

At 17 Carrey moved to Los Angeles and began working at the Comedy Club, where he was discovered by Rodney Dangerfield and signed to open his shows. But two years later Carrey was out of work again after his act failed in Vegas. He didn't seem to be able to make the next step up in the business and became deeply worried. His fear was only increased when, having been invited onto Johnny Carson's *Tonight Show*, he performed his impressions but wasn't invited to join Johnny on the couch for a career-making chat. (For a baby of the family, not being included is one of the worst things that can happen to you.)

Carrey turned his attention toward film, making his debut in *Rubberface* in 1981. But he didn't experience box office success until *Ace Ventura: Pet Detective*—more than ten years later. When he was finally making good money, he moved his parents from Toronto down to his place in Los Angeles. But when the movies he was in failed, his money ran out within a year and he had to send his parents back to Toronto.

But Jim Carrey didn't give up. He drove to the outskirts of Hollywood, looked down on the town, and dreamed of stardom. On a small index card he made out a check for $10 million to himself and postdated it for Thanksgiving 1995. Amazingly, only three days before his father's death in 1994, Carrey was offered $10 million for *The Mask*, and his father was thrilled. When his father died, Carrey slipped his original "check" into his father's pocket before the coffin was closed.

Carrey made headlines with *The Cable Guy*, receiving a record $20 million paycheck. After the success of *The Mask* and *Dumb and Dumber*, both released the same year, Carrey's career took off like a gunshot and he began racking up the awards, including two Golden Globes.

Yet even with all his great success, Jim Carrey suffers from depression. In a *60 Minutes* interview in 2004, he revealed that the inspiration for his funniness was "desperation." He is quoted as saying, "I don't think human beings learn anything without desperation. Desperation is a necessary ingredient to learning anything or creating anything. Period. If you ain't desperate at some point, you ain't interesting."[13]

Interesting is a great word for Jim Carrey—the man best known for his lively physical comedy and almost rubberlike facial expressions. He has taken the most feared act of all human beings—standing up and talking in front of a crowd—and turned it into incredible entertainment. As a baby of the family, he's loving the limelight. (I can relate. When I'm doing a television show, there's nothing that gets me more excited than hearing a producer count down and seeing the stage lights come on.) And along the way, Carrey is helping people lighten up.[14]

> *"If you ain't desperate at some point, you ain't interesting."*
> *—Jim Carrey*

Other babies of the family who became comedians or entertainers are Eddie Murphy, Martin Short, Ellen DeGeneres, Whoopi Goldberg, Jay Leno, Stephen Colbert, Steve Carell, Jon Stewart, Billy Crystal, Danny DeVito, Drew Carey, Chevy Chase, and Steve Martin (note: while he's a baby of his family in ordinal position, he functions as the firstborn son). It's no surprise so many entertainers are babies of the family—keeping people laughing is what babies do best.

If You're a Lastborn . . .

Realize you have the power to make people laugh, to be the life of the party, and to be very persuasive. You can use that power to show off by making a general nuisance of yourself. Or you can turn it around and use it to carve out a successful career in show business, sales, or something similar.

What you need most is a stabilizing influence in your life. It's probably best for you *not* to marry another lastborn. You need a down-to-earth person who can rein in your worst tendencies yet help you fan your best characteristics into flame.

If you're a lastborn, find a responsible firstborn spouse. You may find him or her boring at times, but if you marry someone just like yourself, you're liable to get buried under chaos, unpaid bills, and a big mess. (For more about birth order and favorable marriage matches, see *The Birth Order Book*.) This baby of the family couldn't have picked better when I chose my firstborn wife.

Making the Most of Who You Are

How can you make the most of who you are? Take a survey of your strengths and weaknesses, find a job that fits who you are and how you see the world, then throw yourself into it with gusto. You can succeed by breaking a few rules—Letterman in show business, for instance—but you'll also likely pay a price for doing so.

Whether you're born first, second, third, fourth, or eleventh, you can succeed. You just need to know who you are, build on your strengths, be aware of your weaknesses, and learn to overcome them. And that's what *Have a New You by Friday* is all about.

> *Take a survey of your strengths and weaknesses, find a job that fits who you are and how you see the world, then throw yourself into it with gusto.*

Wednesday

Oh, the Lies We Tell . . . Ourselves

Why your early childhood memories are clues to who you are today, how you came up with your rule book, and what you can do about those sneaky lies you tell yourself about yourself.

If you truly want to understand why you act the way you do, you have one of two options: You can spend thousands of dollars to go to Aluna Moonwalker's five-day "Discover Yourself" workshop in the wilds of Montana, eating legumes and asparagus sandwiches while soaking in a volcanic-ash mud bath after walking across hot coals. *Or* you can stay in the comfort of your home and ask yourself the simple question, "What are my earliest childhood memories, and what do they say about me?"

Hmm . . . now which would you prefer? For nine out of ten of you, I'm guessing you'd rather stay in your easy chair. The rest of you? You need to try out for one of those survival TV shows. The best of luck to you.

Few things unlock the secrets of a person's personality better than exploring the clues, the "private logic," and the reminiscences of early childhood memories. In other words, to understand why you act the way you act as an adult, you need to go back to your childhood. So move over, Dr. Phil, here you go.

Childhood memories aren't about avoiding responsibility; they're about accepting responsibility.

Let me be quick to say, though, that we aren't going to drum up the past so you can avoid all personal responsibility: "My dad called me a sissy when I was eight, so that's why I became a bank robber." While parental actions do affect us, they can affect us in very different ways. For instance, some women who are sexually abused become promiscuous, while others shut down sexually and show no interest in sex at all—even toward their husbands. What makes the difference? The clues are found in each woman's early childhood memories and the life and world perspective she forms as a result.

Childhood memories aren't about *avoiding* responsibility; they're about *accepting* responsibility. They can help you determine what the deepest influences on you were so you can address your tendencies (some good, some bad) as a mature adult.

The Little Boy or Little Girl You Once Were, You Still Are

The basic principle behind early childhood memories is this: the little boy or little girl you once were, you still are. Of course, you've lost some of the freckles and added a few moles. Your face has filled out, and your hair might not be as thick or as blond. But in regard to your personality, your oldest memories are the major indicators of why you believe what you believe, why you do what you do, and why you behave the way you behave.

It's no accident why you hold on to certain memories and have seemingly forgotten others. Your brain is very prejudiced. It holds on to what makes sense and discards what doesn't. If a memory of something that occurred two or three decades ago is still lodged in your mind, there's a reason for it: you remember only those events from early childhood that are consistent with your present view of yourself and the world around you.

Another phrase I use to describe this is your "private logic"—your internal view of yourself and the world. Everyone has a private logic based on their real or imagined experiences, and out of this private logic they write their own unconscious rule book—their belief about how people should respond and why (more about rule books later in this chapter). Some people feel they were picked on and that they always got a bad break, but that may not be true. It may just be the way they perceive their past. But that false perception is still affecting their personality and their view of the world.

If a memory of something that occurred two or three decades ago is still lodged in your mind, there's a reason for it.

Ever wonder why your neighbor always feels like everyone is out to get her? Why she never has anything complimentary to say? One look at her earliest childhood memories would give you a good clue.

Ever wonder why you always seem to jump to the worst side of conclusions about what people are saying about you, before giving them a chance? A look at your earliest childhood memories will reveal a most interesting connecting incident, I'll bet.

When I talk about early childhood memories, I'm talking about memories from age eight years old and younger—second or third grade for most of us. Why so young? Most psychologists agree that by the age of five or six, you've already answered basic

Most psychologists agree that by the age of five or six, you've already answered basic life questions and formed the basis of your personality.

life questions and formed the basis of your personality. Those central questions, "Who am I? What is my place in this world? How will I define good and evil? What is my purpose here?" will be answered ultimately by a private logic that you develop well before puberty.

As you mature, each decision you make and every situation you face is analyzed through this private logic. You justify your actions based on what you believe to be an objective system for understanding the world. So when you go back to your early childhood (age eight and earlier), you're looking at less filtered memories. In fact, you're probably thinking about the memories that *shaped* your current logic, rather than memories that have been clouded and reorganized by your current logic.

Think Back

Right now I want you to try a little exercise. Grab a pen and a piece of paper and find a quiet place. Spend five or ten minutes thinking about and writing down three of your earliest childhood memories. Go ahead—close the book. Don't read any further until you finish this exercise. I'll wait for you until you're back. . . .

Okay, some of you are cheating. Were you always like this? You're a little rebel, aren't you? (Yes, I know. It takes one to know one.) You've kept reading without doing your homework, so I'm going to give you another chance. The surprise won't work if you skip this exercise! Go back and write down three of the first early childhood memories that come to mind. . . .

All right—if you've made it this far, you're either obedient or very, very stubborn.

Let's say that you're a firstborn Great Dane. (By now you ought to know what you are; if not, go back and reread the Monday and Tuesday chapters.) Let me take an educated guess at what you just wrote down. Of the three memories, one or all of the following will appear: a hurtful time, a time when you violated a rule (or you got into trouble), or a memory about achieving something. Or maybe you picked a memory that had height or depth or movement to it: "I remember being on top of a roof and looking down at the ground," or "I remember looking up at my father," etc.

Now let's say you're the youngest, a popular Yorkie. You probably wrote down some happy memories: birthday parties, gifts you received, times when you were in the spotlight. If you wrote down surprises, they were probably positive surprises, when one of your needs was unexpectedly met. Your memories may also contain an "I'll show you" story—a time when someone said you couldn't do something, but that gave you motivation to go out and do it.

If you're a middleborn Irish Setter, you probably remember a time when someone else got in a fight and ruined everything. You may have a few hard-luck stories about how you thought you were going to get a brand-new bike or coat and ended up with an older sibling's hand-me-down. It's very likely that your story will involve you as a negotiator, or perhaps a time when you were dominated and controlled and how angry that made you feel.

If you're an only child Standard Poodle, you probably wrote down a hurtful time when you didn't meet someone's high standards, a time when you were praised for your organizational or analytical skills, or a time when someone you knew made something, but you couldn't help looking at it and thinking, *Yeah, that's really good . . . but I could have done it better.*

Am I right?

Ninety percent of the time, I will be.

How can a stranger who has never met you, talked to you, or even seen you come so close to pinning down your early childhood memories? It's simple. You remember the things that are consistent with your private logic. Since I've counseled hundreds of firstborns and just as many lastborns, not to mention middles, I know exactly what most of you are thinking. Scary, huh?

Several years ago I was at a huge annual book convention—a weeklong whirl of book publicity for publishers, editors, salespeople, and writers. After full days of signing books, giving interviews, and meeting with publishers, I started to feel tired and, I admit, a little bored. (Remember that lastborns like me are a party continually waiting to happen. Doing the same thing day in and day out just isn't our forte.) I needed a pick-me-up, so I headed for the group of salespeople and pulled up a chair.

For me, the fun was only beginning.

One sales guy politely asked me what my next book project was going to be. I was only too happy to oblige him. "I'm writing a book on why you are the way you are, helping people to understand their personality."

He raised a brow. "How are you going to do that?"

"Well, for instance, I'll take them through their early childhood memories."

He scoffed (nicely, but it was still a scoff). "I don't know if I believe in that early childhood memory stuff."

I could tell by his cynical, analytical nature and his impeccable dress that I was talking to a firstborn, so I decided to have a little more fun. "Well, they're pretty powerful indicators," I said. "In fact, why don't you give me an early childhood memory of yours?"

He just stared.

"Better yet," I said, "let *me* give you your early childhood memories."

Now the sales guy was looking at me like I was absolutely nuts.

I turned a card over and wrote down three general memories: achievement; breaking a rule; and depth, movement, or height.

"All right," I said. "Think about three childhood memories, and then describe the first one for me. They need to be before you turned eight years old."

"I remember being on my grandfather's farm, sitting on top of a hayloft, looking out from there."

"Bingo," I said and pointed to what I had written on the card.

His jaw dropped open in astonishment. He looked further up my list and then was really surprised. "Hey," he said, "you got my second memory too!" He then talked about breaking one of his grandfather's rules.

Why could I "predict" those three general memories for that salesman? Because birth order and memories are usually closely aligned. If I know someone's birth order, I can usually predict the general nature of their memories. When I appeared on a show in Dallas, I invited callers to give me their early childhood memories. After hearing them, I told the callers their birth order. The callers and the host were amazed, but in all honesty, there's not that much to it. In fact, once you're done with this book, you should be able to do the same thing.

While the fact that our memories can be conditioned by our birth order may be troubling to some, it can be absolutely exhilarating to others: "You mean I've *learned* to become the person I am?"

Yes! You are the way you are because of the choices you have made in response to your surrounding environment.

So what's the good news? You can change.

If you're a flaw-picking, cynical, abrasive person who is eating up more friends than you can replace, you can change. If you're a happy-go-lucky kind of person but also ditzy and irresponsible, you can develop the necessary good qualities to balance your

What Do You Remember?

Following are the general memories each birth order will have.

Firstborns
- achieving something
- breaking a rule
- a memory of depth, movement, or height

Onlies
- failing to meet someone's high standards
- being praised for their organizational or analytical skills
- knowing they could have done something better than someone else

Middleborns
- being a negotiator
- being dominated or controlled
- wearing hand-me-downs

Lastborns
- being in the spotlight
- a surprise
- an I'll-show-you story

adorable absentmindedness. Once you understand what makes you tick, you can forge new patterns of behavior and remake your personality. In short, you can become a new you!

"But I Don't Have Any Memories"

Talking about early childhood memories usually gets a room buzzing, but there are always a few who stand up and insist, "But Dr. Leman, I don't have any childhood memories."

> *What's the good news? You can change.*

Yes, you do. Though many of us wish we could push "Rewind"—or even better, "Delete"—in our brains, the fact is, we can't. What you have done, seen, experienced, and felt is recorded in the deep recesses of your mind. Just because you have a hard time getting at the memories doesn't mean they aren't in there.

There are a couple of exceptions, of course. In the case of severe trauma—extreme abuse or overwhelming tragedy—the brain does sometimes call into play a very effective coping mechanism called *repression*. Repression, as well as denial, has its place. It allows putting off dealing with traumatic events until later in life. If you've undergone a traumatic experience in the past, this book cannot replace professional counseling. It can aid in your journey but not complete your journey. Please go after the help you need.

But for the rest of you, there are a few ways to help restore memories that have seemingly been sent to the recycle bin in your mind.

Relax

Bringing up memories is best done with a quiet mind. The reason some people blot out their childhood is that they are so busy today they just can't slow down to take time to think. They're so used to operating at maximum capacity that taking even a short time-out feels wrong. If you're of this temperament, find a quiet place, turn off the TV, and do some introspective thinking.

Ask Yourself Questions

In order to begin to understand your private logic and how it formed, prompt your memories with these questions:

- What is your earliest school-related memory? Can you think of a teacher you liked (or disliked), a classmate who was a close friend, or a bully who mistreated you?
- Do you have any memories of doing something alone with one of your parents? If so, what was one of them?
- How did your family spend its leisure time? Do you recall any summer vacations or special weekend outings?
- How did your family spend holidays? Do you remember a particularly painful (or happy) birthday or Christmas?
- Did you have any pets growing up? Did you ever turn to your pet for solace or to talk out a problem?
- What was your neighborhood like? Think about some of the families who lived near you. Any events come to mind?
- Where did you sit at the table? What was mealtime like at your home? Did you even have mealtimes together?
- Describe your early childhood bedroom. What was on the walls? What did you keep near your bed? Did you ever hide anything in your bedroom?
- Who taught you how to swim? How to ride a bike? How to catch a baseball?
- How were you disciplined?

- If your family was one of faith, how did they act at church or synagogue compared to how they acted at home the rest of the time?

- Do thoughts of your childhood room make you feel comforted, sad, lonely, or scared?

Talk to Your Siblings

Sometimes talking over past vacations, holidays, and family stories with other siblings can do wonders to release your own memories. Be careful, though. Sometimes family stories can take on the nature of legends, and truth can get rewritten. Make sure the memory is *your* memory and it really happened. Use your siblings more as people who can help provoke your memories than as people who can fill in the details.

Look at Family Mementos

Perhaps even more helpful than talking to your siblings is looking through old photographs or watching home movies. A picture of a lamp, a teddy bear, or an old outfit can release any number of early childhood memories. Even the aroma of an item from your past can release memories.

Self-Check

1. Look back at the "What to Do on Monday" checklist (see page 58). What have you done differently in your life since Monday?
2. Look back at the "What to Do on Tuesday" checklist (see page 93). What have you done differently in your life since Tuesday?
3. Are you succeeding in becoming a new you? If so, great! Forge ahead. If not, face the lie within you that says, "I will never succeed at this, so why try?"

Get Specific

General memories won't work for this exercise. "I always liked to ride my bike after school" isn't a memory; it's a generalization. A memory has to refer to a specific event that occurred at a specific time, even if you can't place the exact date. For example: "One time when I was riding my bike after school, I crashed into the family station wagon and got into trouble." That's a memory. Keep reaching for specific events.

Warning: Memories Can Lie like Dogs

If you know anything about baseball, you probably know at least a little something about Joe DiMaggio, one of baseball's all-time greatest players. What you may not know is that DiMaggio had a younger brother named Dom who was nearly as good a player—and some say an even better fielder. Casey Stengel once said, "With the possible exception of his brother Dom, Joe is the best outfielder in the league."[1]

While Dom was excellent in the outfield and an accomplished hitter, he could never quite match his older brother's dominance at the plate. No one could. In 1941 Joe made history as he tied Willie Keeler's record for consecutive games with a hit (44). Joe needed just one more game to break the record and have it all to himself.

As fate would have it, game 45 was played against the Boston Red Sox—Dom's team. Dom often told the story of being out in the field when a long line drive leaped off Joe's bat in the first inning. Dom recalls making a leaping catch and depriving Joe of a hit, which he says was like driving a stake through Joe's heart. "As we crossed paths in the outfield, I tried to avoid making eye contact with him, but he was staring me down," Dom recalls. "If looks could kill, I would have dropped dead on the spot."[2]

This incident says a lot about sibling rivalry, younger brother–older brother relations, and Dom's personality in particular. There's a problem with this story, however. Dom DiMaggio didn't make that catch—Stan Spence did. Look it up in the record books; it's right there. But you couldn't convince Dom that he wasn't the one who put his brother's streak in jeopardy more than 60 years ago. (For all you baseball buffs, Joe grounded out in his second at bat but homered in his third to keep the streak alive, which eventually ended at 56.)

Memories are by no means infallible. In fact, they lie like dogs. Years ago, my good friend Moonhead and I were in midget league baseball (not to be confused with Little League, which hadn't been invented yet—which just goes to show how old I am). Moonhead and I have been friends since we were both three years old, and every year we have an annual fight over the "fact" that as manager of our baseball team, he didn't give me a hat. We didn't have full uniforms back in those days, but we did get a shirt and a cap, and Moonhead's job was to make sure I got mine. But since I missed a couple practices (when my family went on the only vacation we ever had), Moonhead said I wouldn't get a hat.

To be fair, Moonhead disputes my story. He insists that he gave me a hat and I probably lost it. But I'm just as convinced that he's lying. It's been 55 years, and stubborn old Moonhead still won't admit he's wrong.

> *Only one of us is right. The other one is lying.*

"Leman," he says, "you know me. I'm not a petty guy. It isn't my nature to do something like that."

"Oh yeah?" I say. "Sounds to me like a classic case of denial. The truth is too painful for you to admit. Look at this!" I take out my trump card, an old team picture that clearly shows me as the only player with a different cap.

"That doesn't prove anything," Moonhead says. "You're a last-born. You were losing things all the time."

> **How My Life Changed**
>
> When I first heard you talk about childhood memories on the radio, I thought, *Oh no, another quack.* But your words kept coming to mind. So even though I was still skeptical of the idea, I took a crack at it. I was stunned at what I remembered. Now I know why I try so hard not to rock the boat (it's been the mantra of my life) and I never seem to get anywhere in life. I told three friends about your book *What Your Childhood Memories Say about You . . . and What You Can Do about It,* and we're reading a chapter a week and talking about it over coffee on Thursday nights. Thanks for opening my eyes to why I am what I am. I guess the rest is up to me.
>
> Madison, Virginia

"It does too prove something," I counter. "It proves you punished me for nothing and made me go an entire season wearing a different-colored hat."

"Leman, you get things in your head. What do you psychologists call it? Transposition or something like that?"

What strikes me about this annual argument (except for the fact that Moonhead still won't admit he's wrong) is that two grown men can be so adamant about something that happened so long ago. Both of us are absolutely, positively convinced that we are right, but there's just one thing for certain: only one of us is right. The other one is lying.

See how easy it is to manufacture and edit memories from childhood? The *Journal of Experimental Psychology* found in a study that "people unconsciously tamper with their own memories, inventing causes for events they see around them to help make sense of things."[3] For example, a study in *Psychology and Marketing* found that 35 percent claimed to have shaken hands with Bugs Bunny on a past visit to the Magic Kingdom.[4] Of course, Bugs is a Warner Brothers creation, not a Disney character. No child has ever shaken Bugs Bunny's hand inside the happiest place on earth, even though a lot of people "remember" doing so.

Mark Reinitz, a psychologist at the University of Puget Sound in Tacoma, Washington, explains, "Memory isn't a record. It's an interpretation to a large extent."[5] But this doesn't discount our childhood memories. It provides all the more reason to analyze them. A false memory may yield even more understanding than a true one. Psychologist Elizabeth Loftus says, "Memory is malleable for a reason. It helps us remember ourselves in a more positive light."[6]

> *A false memory may yield even more understanding than a true one.*

As you learn to look objectively at your memories (what are these memories really saying?), you begin to understand the private logic by which you approach life. Once you've begun building a pool of memories, you can begin analyzing them to help you understand your assumed rule book (again, we'll cover this later in the chapter). To help you in this exercise, allow me to share one or two memories of my own.

The Wayward Cub

I grew up with the nickname "Cub," or "Cubby." My father gave me this name when I was just 11 days old. He picked me up in his hands, chuckled, and said, "This boy looks just like a little bear cub." (Take a look at my author picture on this book, and you might agree I still do.)

Of course, I have no memory of my dad doing that, but being called "Cubby" shaped me in many ways. As I stated earlier, any name with a *y* or *ie* ending—Bobby, Jimmy, Annie, Suzy—usually indicates lastborn status. A firstborn would normally change his or her name to Robert, James, Ann, or Susan. Being called by a kid-sounding name affects how you view yourself. That's why some memories stick in a very vivid way.

I doubt I'll ever forget when I was in Cub Scouts. During one den meeting, that week's den mother brought out some of her famous peanut butter cookies. Unfortunately, she served them on a very expensive china plate.

As a young kid, if I ate lunch at noon, I'd be hungry again by 1:30 or 2:00. It was well into the afternoon, and I smelled those cookies before I saw them. When she placed the cookies near the edge of the table, one cookie in particular caught my eye. Bigger than the rest, with just the right amount of sugar sprinkled on top, that cookie practically had my name written on it.

The challenge, of course, was that there were six or seven other grubby little Scouts who saw the plate the same time I did. That plate had barely touched the table when my hand went out to grab the prized cookie. But my enthusiasm got the better of me, and my elbow sent the plate flying. It was the worst three seconds of my life, watching that china plate take off from the table and go hurtling toward its demise on the hard floor below.

There was a crash, a gasp, and then a terrible scolding: "Cubby Leman! Every time you walk into this house, something gets broken!"

To make matters worse, the plate turned out to be an heirloom—it had belonged to the den mother's great-grandmother and could never be replaced. Now, I ask you, what den mother in her right mind would serve cookies to a bunch of rowdy boys on an heirloom china plate? Of course, I didn't have that kind of reasoning as a kid.

> *I grew up with the nickname "Cub," or "Cubby." Being called by a kid-sounding name affects how you view yourself.*

Looking back as an adult, I can understand why she would lash out after losing something with such sentimental value. (Though why she couldn't have served them on a paper plate or a plastic plate that would have a longer shelf life with boys is still beyond me.) But as a kid, I knew there were any number of mothers who could have said the same thing: "Cubby Leman! Every time you walk into this house, something gets broken!"

Eventually I got thrown out of Scouts. The final straw came the day our den had planned a big tour that required a minimum number of participants. I had signed up to attend, but something happened that morning and I decided not to go. (That's a typical lastborn trait, by the way—it wasn't convenient, so I blew it off.)

> *I got thrown out of Scouts.*

As it turned out, my not showing up meant that no one could participate, because without me they didn't have enough people. The whole den lost out. If I had called and canceled, the den master at least could have notified everyone before they showed up. My lack of common courtesy made everyone lose half a day, and the Scout leader had had enough. I was gone.

Another memory has a similar theme. My mom used to subject our Christmas tree to some ugly antique Norwegian ornaments she had inherited from my grandmother. What's worse, Mom wouldn't let me get the nice shiny bulbs from the dime store because our tree was too full of those ugly antique ones, so I did what any enterprising young boy would do: I took out my pellet gun and had target practice.

You should have seen those ornaments burst apart! I had never seen anything like it. There was a very satisfying "pop" when they were hit, and then the coolest shatter you've ever seen. Before I knew it, I had just about cleared the tree.

As I looked at my work with satisfaction, it suddenly dawned on me that I was looking at quite a mess and that my mom, who didn't share my opinion on the aesthetic value of these bulbs, might be less than pleased with someone for shooting them up. (Do I hear some readers saying, "Leman, I'm glad you're not my kid"?)

I gathered up my gun and fled the scene. About 20 minutes later, I heard a shriek and ran into the living room. "What is it, Mom?"

I asked, looking horrified, shocked, and amazed that such a thing could have happened in the peaceful Leman abode.

"Cubby!" my mom yelled. "Did you do this?"

"Wasn't me, Mom," I lied. "Must have been the cat."

Mom bought my explanation, and the poor cat paid a heavy price. My mom was pretty easy to fool. When people would ask her about me, she'd say, "Oh, he's always such a *good* boy," only because she never knew the half of it. The frequent trips she took to the principal's office ought to have given her a clue, but Mom always believed the best of me in spite of the evidence.

So what do these memories mean? As I've already stated, you remember things that are consistent with how you view life. If I were counseling myself, I'd say, "Kevin, you see yourself as a rule breaker, a rebel, don't you?"

I certainly do. One of my more common thoughts growing up was, *Oh, crud, I'm in trouble again.* I was always in trouble for *something*. Consequently, rules don't mean that much to me—even today. I've broken rules all my life. For instance, in the academic world, there's an unwritten law that you're not supposed to get all your degrees at the same school. You're supposed to go to one school for your bachelor's degree, a different school for your master's, and yet a third school for your doctorate. Occasionally you'll see people get their master's and doctorate at the same place, but not that often. To get all three degrees from the same institution, however, is unheard of.

Except that I did it. I liked the University of Arizona, and I didn't want to go anywhere else—so I didn't!

Even today, I continue my quest to break the rules. More than a few passengers have turned their heads my way when I've boarded an airplane in the dead of winter wearing shorts. Can I help it if

> *I was always in trouble for something. Consequently, rules don't mean that much to me—even today.*

the rest of the country doesn't have the good sense to move to Tucson when it gets cold everywhere else?

Legalists who live only by rules, many of which are made up by humans, have always driven me up the wall. Now, my faith is very important to me. Being faithful to my wife and family is near the top of my list. But following rules for their own sake, such as you don't chew gum or go bowling, you watch movies only with G ratings, you don't speak about certain subjects (especially my favorite subject, sex!)—I have no tolerance for that stunted line of thinking.

> *Even today, I continue my quest to break the rules. More than a few passengers have turned their heads my way when I've boarded an airplane in the dead of winter wearing shorts.*

Throughout my publishing career, more than one editor has taken offense at something I've said in a manuscript and has written me a note about it. Some writers I know would be mortified to receive such a note. Me? I take it as a badge of honor. If what I write doesn't upset a few people, I don't feel like I've done my job. What else is a book or a talk supposed to do if not rock the boat a little? If everyone agrees with everything I say, why am I wasting my time saying it?

Do you see how my memories shape who I am as an adult? I'm no longer breaking plates (well, occasionally), but the mind-set is still there.

Breaking rules and having the label of a rebel doesn't bother me. I'm comfortable with it. I use it to my advantage. I see it as one of the unique things that makes me who I am. Instead of running from it, I try to capitalize on it and put it to good use. When I'm speaking to certain audiences, I don't mind pushing the envelope. But I also try very hard not to bust that envelope wide open. I want to respect and honor the people who invited me.

Early childhood memories provide the key to unlocking the mystery of why you see things the way you do, why certain things bug you that don't bug others, and why some things comfort you that frighten others. They reveal your unspoken assumptions about the way you think life ought to go . . . and not go.

If you identify and analyze your early childhood memories, you'll be amazed at what you find out about yourself and the private logic through which you see life. That private logic is what forms your personal "rule book"—the unspoken assumptions that can control the rest of your life (especially if you're not aware of them).

> *Early childhood memories reveal your unspoken assumptions about the way you think life ought to go . . . and not go.*

What's in Your Rule Book?

One person drives his car directly into the Employee of the Month parking space even though he's not an employee and there's an empty stall right next to it. Another person passes up the space even though doing so means walking a hundred yards in the rain.

Why?

One college grad sends out 50 résumés and doesn't get a single request for an interview, so she follows up each silent response with a personal visit to the company and ends up getting five job offers. Another woman sends out three résumés, receives three rejections, and quits looking, then takes an entry-level job with her father's company—even though she has a four-year degree and is seriously overqualified for the position.

Why?

One father takes a very laid-back approach to parenting. His grade-school kids go to bed only when they get tired, even if that means staying up until 10 or 11 at night, and they all have permission to eat whenever they want to as long as they clean up their mess. Another dad treats bedtime like a divine mandate. If his eight-year-old isn't in bed by 8:30, she'll be grounded the next day after school. And once dinner is over, there is absolutely no way any food is going into her mouth until breakfast is served the next morning.

Why?

In each scenario, the people are acting according to rule books that make sense to them. One rule book says, "The day is more fun when you bend the rules. Life is too short to let other people tell you what to do." People who live by this rule book enjoy getting others upset by deliberately flaunting their independence. They park in areas where they're not supposed to park, they say things that might shock others, and they sometimes dress in a way that's sure to garner attention.

Another group lives by the motto, "If I break a rule—any rule— the punishment will be severe and far greater than any enjoyment I might get out of doing what I want. Therefore, I won't break any rule, no matter what." Such a person is likely to be unusually submissive, the kind that producers have great fun with on *Candid Camera*. They'll do anything you ask them to if they sense you have the authority to ask them to do it. Simply put up a sign and they'll obey it.

> *Your rule book is a very individual thing, and it governs virtually everything you do.*

In the example about two college graduates, the first woman is living by a rule book that says, "I always find a way. When people tell me I can't do something, that just makes me want to prove them wrong." Under this guideline for living, rejection doesn't act as a deterrent; it's a stimulus. It gets her motivated. The second woman has a rule book that says, "Every time I stick my neck out, it gets cut off. It hurts more to be rejected than anything else, so I'm not going to try anymore." A person who believes this to be true will give up at the first sign of struggle and settle in at

Daddy's company without really trying to prove her worth in the outside world.

These rule books are shaped by our responses to our childhood memories, our upbringing, and our birth order. Rule books within families will usually have some similarities, but they'll also have marked differences. Ultimately your rule book is a very individual thing, and it governs virtually everything you do.

> ### Lies You Tell Yourself
>
> I wouldn't be this way if my parents hadn't done _____.
>
> If _____ wouldn't have happened, I wouldn't have done _____.
>
> I wouldn't have done _____ if my parents hadn't done _____.
>
> It's all their fault.
>
> I don't deserve it. I'm not worth it.

Look back at the piece of paper where you wrote down your three early childhood memories. You'll evaluate those memories in a couple different ways: first, to explore what kind of parents you had; and second, to understand your personality.

Memories of Your Parents

I'll say it bluntly. If you can look back at your parents and smile, remembering time spent together with joy, you are truly blessed indeed. Some of you reading this book won't be able to recall a single positive thing about your life growing up. Others of you will remember two or three positive events in the midst of a life of uncertainty. Some of you have grown up with a critical-eyed parent, and that criticism has become a part of you that never makes you feel good enough, no matter what you do. Still others of you grew up with parents who snowplowed your road of life, not holding you accountable for anything. Then you walked in the jaws of life and found out life wasn't quite as wonderful as it was at home with dear ol' Mom and Dad watching out for you.

Your parents have a lot to do with what makes you "you." But the good news is, they don't have to have the last word . . . unless you give them the power to do so.

Authoritarian Parents

If your parents were unduly harsh and subscribed to the lay-down-the-law-and-take-no-prisoners approach to parenting, you probably have memories about getting in trouble for breaking the rules. If you grew up with a lot of rules, you probably felt like you were always breaking at least one of them.

> *Your parents have a lot to do with what makes you "you." But the good news is, they don't have to have the last word . . . unless you give them the power to do so.*

Mark grew up with very strict religious parents. He wasn't allowed to shop on Sundays, but his parents had never really explained why.

One hot summer Sunday, Mark's best buddy, Jimmy, rode his bike up to Mark's house, peddling as if his life were in danger.

"What's up?" Mark asked.

"They just got Brooks Robinson's cup in at the 7-Eleven!" Jimmy responded.

Mark was a die-hard Orioles fan, and the 7-Eleven had pictures of major league baseball players on their plastic cups that year. He couldn't wait to get a cup with his favorite third baseman on it.

He ran into the house to get his money when his mom asked him what the hurry was. All of a sudden, Mark remembered it was Sunday and that his mom wouldn't appreciate him spending money at any store, not even a 7-Eleven. He thought quickly, then blurted out, "Uh, Jimmy just captured a snake at his house. I'm going over to see it."

"Okay, but be back by 5:00. We're eating an early dinner tonight."

Mark jumped on his bike and rode with Jimmy to the 7-Eleven. He could taste that cherry Slurpee even before he touched it. The cool drink felt good in his hand, and boy, what a thrill to see Brooks Robinson's picture and a stamped autograph on the cup! Just as Mark and Jimmy walked out of the convenience store, though, Mark's next-door neighbors—members of his family's church—walked by.

"Why, Mark, what are you doing here on a Sunday?"

Suddenly that cold Slurpee felt like a death warrant. There was no way Mark could hide the evidence in his hand, and he knew without asking that the first thing

> *Suddenly that cold Slurpee felt like a death warrant.*

these neighbors would do when they got home would be to talk to his parents. He dropped that Slurpee into the trash—prized Robinson cup and all—and sadly walked his bike home.

While this story tugs at the heartstrings, what's most significant is that Mark was in his thirties, still haunted by that memory, when he told me about it. Both of his parents had died—but their style of parenting was still very much with him.

Authoritarian parents also have a tendency to withhold emotional warmth and involvement. When Victoria was six years old, she drew a picture for her mother. She had overheard her mother say how much she enjoyed a good sunset, so her daughter worked the better part of two days on drawing just such a scene. Finally, when she thought she had it just right, she proudly showed it to her mom, who was busy cleaning the kitchen and who seemed to resent the interruption. Mom said, "That's nice, dear," and immediately put the picture down. The girl was hurt beyond words, but not nearly as much as she was two days later when she was putting out the trash and found the picture crumpled up in the garbage can.

Doesn't your heart go out to that little girl? Now consider that the woman who told me that story was in her forties . . . but she

139

still remembered that event and feels the pain as if she were six years old again!

If you had very authoritarian parents, you're probably going to display some of the following personality characteristics. Keep in mind that some of these traits contradict each other—we all respond differently when facing the same type of pressure—but these are the most typical responses to overly strict parenting:

- You'll wait until your teenage or college years to rebel and then flaunt your independence in the face of virtually any authority.
- You'll become extremely compliant, quiet, and cooperative.
- You'll go out of your way to be obnoxious. You'll start stupid quarrels, get into lots of fights, and be very rude and abrasive.
- You'll lack the ability to be spontaneous and to be an independent thinker. You'll have very little creativity. Instead, you'll see everything in black and white.
- You'll rely on other people to make decisions for you. You'll feel like you need to be controlled, like you have to have some authority directly over you. Otherwise life is too scary.

Permissive Parents

Even as a seven-year-old, Doug knew he could do no wrong. His parents never held him accountable, and they even frequently went out of their way to defend him. Doug could get away with anything. That's why he thought he'd help himself out at the local junior fishing derby. After he pulled a bass out of the lake, he dropped a bunch of sinkers down its throat to increase the weight.

The judges weren't naive. They had seen every trick invented and then some. They quickly discovered the sinkers and disqualified the boy's entry.

The father was furious—but at the judges, not at Doug. He thought they should just pour out the sinkers and weigh the empty fish. His son had made an error in judgment, but why disqualify him for a childish mistake that probably every kid had tried at least once?

Another classic case of a very permissive parent is golfer John Daly's father. John Daly is well known as a troubled soul. Though he had some remarkable early successes on the professional golf tour, he has had even more struggles. To begin with, he had an ongoing problem with his weight for years, yet one of his favorite breakfasts was biscuits with chocolate gravy. (Recently, however, the chubby guy on the golf course lost 115 pounds, "after a surgery and changing his lifestyle that had him up to 280 pounds."[7]) His desire for alcohol is so strong that he once drove away from a rehab unit, knowing that doing so would cost him a $3-million-a-year endorsement contract with Callaway Golf. He has run up over $2 million in gambling debts and has been divorced twice. To help tame his volcanic temper, which has led to his arrest for domestic disturbance on several occasions, doctors have put him on just about every manic-depressive drug imaginable: lithium, Prozac, Xanax, Paxil. You name it, he's been on it.[8]

I could go on and on, but I think you get the point. Daly is a troubled man. Yet when his dad was interviewed, he couldn't understand why Daly's sponsors made such a fuss. "And they're controllin' [his] life! Here's a guy who really doesn't have any problems, except that he likes to drink. . . . OK, John had a few drinks and hit some golf balls maybe where he shouldn't. Because of that, they put him in rehab?"[9]

Look, any man who has had several arrests for domestic disturbance, is running up million-dollar gambling debts, and has twice called friends threatening to commit suicide certainly has a few problems—more than just "liking to drink." But some parents just can't see the trouble their kids are really getting into—and they remain lenient to their dying day, much to their child's harm.

If your parents were too permissive, I bet you have memories of getting away with something but maybe feeling a little guilty about it afterward. Your memories probably also center around getting presents, having parties, taking trips, being absolutely spoiled at Christmas, and indulging in other activities. While such parenting might allow you to have what you think is a little extra fun as a kid, it can also reap disastrous results for your personality as an adult.

If your parents were too permissive, your rule book probably contains some of the following:

- You have a tendency to be extremely self-centered. Because you always got your own way, you have what others see as an amazing lack of empathy and consideration for others.
- You come off as socially adept, but you lack the internal ability to truly care about others and develop deep relationships. Therefore, most of your friends are casual friends who know they can't count on you.
- If you see something you want, you do your best to get it, regardless of what it costs or what the consequences of your actions may be.
- You have a judgmental spirit and a critical tongue.
- You've probably picked up at least one addiction. It might be gambling, overeating, sex, or drinking, but in one area you show little or no restraint.

Critical Parents

One of the sadder cases I've worked on concerned a family with an overly critical dad. His son Bobby was a pretty good ballplayer. He wasn't the best hitter on the team, but he did bat leadoff, which meant the coach saw him as one of the most reliable and consistent batters to get on base. The boy's dad never got around to watching any of his son's games. He worked long hours and demanded as much from himself as he did from his kids. But after Bobby begged all spring, his dad finally agreed to leave work early (6:00 p.m.) and make it to his son's game.

"Will you make me proud, Son?" the dad asked that morning.

"I will, Dad," Bobby replied.

There was something in the dad's question that unleashed a number of negative emotions in the boy. The question was really more of a command: "Don't embarrass me, don't let me down, don't make me look like a fool." The dad obviously had his own insecurity problems, and these problems were leaking into his parenting.

The boy was excited that his dad would finally see him play, but he was getting more anxious as the day wore on. After all, the very best hitters in Little League scarcely batted more than .400. Just what was his dad expecting him to do? How would his dad react to a strikeout?

Finally, 6:00 arrived. As the leadoff hitter, Bobby was the very first batter in the game. He looked at his dad just before he got to the plate and felt his stomach flip. There was no word of encouragement from his dad. Rather, he received a warning glare, and every negative phrase this boy had heard growing up came hurtling back into his mind. He barely knew which end of the bat to hold by the time he reached the plate.

The first pitch hit the dirt in front of the plate. To the coach's astonishment, his leadoff hitter swung at—and of course missed—this terrible pitch. The crowd groaned. The next pitch was high, almost over the batter's head. Again, Bobby swung. Again, the entire crowd groaned.

The boy, in a panic now, tried to gather his strength.

"All right now, Bobby," the coach called out. "Make him pitch to you."

Bobby nodded and stepped back into the box. *Don't swing at just anything*, he told himself, terrified that he would strike out.

That's why he left the bat on his shoulder as the pitcher delivered a fastball right down the middle of the plate, a pitch that Bobby normally would have sent careening into center field.

"Strike three, you're ouuuutttt!" the umpire yelled.

Three pitches. Three strikes.

Bobby turned fearfully toward the stands, only to see his dad's back as he walked away. Bobby's dad wasn't going to stay if his son was going to embarrass him.

> *Bobby turned fearfully toward the stands, only to see his dad's back as he walked away.*

Adults who had critical parents often report memories in which they are laughed at for making a simple, childish mistake—misspelling an easy word or incorrectly answering a rather simple math formula.

If your parents were too critical, I bet you can relate to some of the following:

- You often procrastinate, making the excuse that there's not enough time, but in truth you're simply afraid to have anything you do evaluated.
- You carry a lot of guilt and negative self-speak. You criticize yourself mercilessly for the smallest mistake, and you have a hard time forgetting any instance where you've let yourself or someone else down.
- You never believe that you truly measure up. You always feel like you're letting someone down, that you could be doing it a little better. Even when others praise your work, you think they're only being nice.
- You have very little self-confidence and almost no self-esteem.
- You don't picture yourself as a success. Even if you stumble onto financial or vocational success, you always expect the

---

How My Life Changed

My mom was always pushing me when I was young, telling me that if I didn't do everything 100 percent, I'd never get anywhere in life . . . and that I'd be stuck in a dead-end job, just like her. I left home as soon as I turned 18, just to get away from her harping. (I sure can't blame my dad for leaving.)

Now I'm living in my own apartment and working in a grocery store to make ends meet. When I was feeling really down about myself, a good friend let me borrow her book *What Your Childhood Memories Say about You*, and the phrase "Do memories = you today?" really stuck with me. That's when I realized how hurt I was that my mom thought I'd never turn out to be anything, and that I was helping my mom's prediction come true instead of trying to do the best for myself.

Last week I enrolled at a community college. I'm going to take two classes a semester until I finish my college degree. For me, that's a huge step in the right direction.

Jane, Oregon

---

other shoe to drop. You're just waiting for the bottom to fall out so you'll be exposed as the loser you know you are.

Authoritative Parents

Chances are, you're reading this book because you had an authoritarian parent, a permissive parent, or a critical parent. But there's another type of parent. If you had an *authoritative* parent (few do), you had a jump start on everyone else—and you would be in the minority of the people reading this book.

Authoritative parents tend to ask their child the facts about a situation before they jump to conclusions. They look out for their child's welfare yet allow the child to experience the consequences of his or her behavior. They give the child age-appropriate choices and establish guidelines for behavior by working with him or her. They provide the child with decision-making opportunities and develop consistent, loving discipline. They hold the child accountable and let reality be the teacher. They convey respect, self-worth, and love to the child and therefore enhance his or her self-esteem.

Was this your experience at home? If so, blessings are heaped upon you because you have a balanced home foundation to draw from in making your decisions. Your parents not only made wise choices, but they probably helped you on your journey to make wise choices. You're the person least likely to need this book. Hand it to a friend!

What's the difference between the styles of parenting? Any extreme style of parenting will cause children to rebel. With a permissive parent, there are no guidelines, and children flounder. With the authoritarian or critical parent, everything is heavy-handed. The wise parent finds the middle ground.[10]

Now What about *Your* Traits?

We've looked at your memories in relation to how your parents treated you. Now let's look at memories that reveal your own tendencies. Your parents' style of child rearing has certainly shaped you, but you also made some choices about how you would respond. In addition to understanding how you were raised, you need to get a feel for what traits you developed in response.

Keep in mind that none of the four "labels" we'll talk about next are necessarily bad. For instance, even being a controller can be a good trait. I know a lot of nurses who are wonderful controllers, and I'm glad they take charge. If they didn't, those of us who sometimes have to go into a hospital would be in trouble!

The important thing is figuring out who you've become in response to your memories so that you can change the parts of yourself you aren't happy with. Are you a controller? A pleaser? A charmer? Or a victim?

The Controller

A controlling memory is one in which you're in charge—you're arranging the neighborhood game, you're the kid called on in the case of an emergency, you're bringing order to chaos. Controlling memories are particularly common with Great Dane temperaments.

If I notice control-related early childhood memories in your past, I can make some basic assumptions about who you are. It's likely that you place high expectations on yourself and on others. You may prefer to work alone, because then no one can mess up what you're doing. You probably hate surprises because you never want to be caught off guard or ill prepared. You draw great satisfaction from accomplishing something, are probably pretty competitive, and prefer to be the person in charge. In your view, people tend to be a little too laid-back—if they don't want to win, they shouldn't play the game. I wouldn't be surprised if you have a little problem with your temper.

> *It's likely that you place high expectations on yourself and on others.*

I worked with Dick, a firstborn who had control-related early childhood memories. He was a classic textbook Great Dane in many regards. His wife, Terri, had made a terrible mistake for his forty-fifth birthday party—she decided to surprise him. Had Terri consulted me, I would have told her a surprise party is the last thing she should have considered, but as a Yorkie, she thought a surprise birthday party would be fun.

Strike one.

Because Terri had to prepare the rented hall for the party, she arranged for their teenage son, Ryan, to convince his dad that he needed a ride to Grange Hall for a weekend youth function. Well, Terri didn't realize that her Great Dane husband had plans for the day—he was finally going to get the fence stained.

When Ryan went outside to request a ride, Dick was wearing an old paint shirt, colorful and outdated shorts, scummy tennis shoes, and a paint hat. Ryan suggested that maybe his dad would like to change, but Dick looked at his son like he was crazy: "Why do I need to change to give you a lift to the hall?"

Ryan was faced with a dilemma—either spoil the surprise or let his dad drive him to the party wearing that ridiculous outfit. The boy decided to maintain the surprise and let his dad come dressed as he was.

> *Do your family a favor. Have a frank talk with them.*

Strike two.

Dick showed up looking ridiculous, and Ryan convinced him that he needed to walk into the hall. By that time, Dick was suspicious. When he realized his friends and family members were waiting to yell, "Surprise!" he was far more agitated than pleased. He hated being put in a situation for which he wasn't dressed appropriately. Besides, he had left the stain and paint brushes out, and all he could think about was the half-finished project at home.

Strike three.

If you're a Great Dane firstborn with controlling memories, do your family a favor. Have a frank talk with them. Explain how you like things to be run. Give them a chance to understand you and to avoid making mistakes that would seem obvious to you but may not be to them.

The Pleaser

Pleaser memories are most common among women. I've known a few men with pleaser memories, but this is one category that's definitely gender biased. Maybe a little girl tried to help her dad by painting the house, but she made a mess of it. Perhaps she tried to help him shine his shoes, and she missed a spot. Or maybe she even attempted to mow the lawn and ran over some flowers by mistake. Other pleaser memories end with the child taking blame—whether or not she was actually at fault.

I see pleaser memories most often with Irish Setter middleborns and compliant firstborns. Usually these people lack confidence, live with a good bit of fear (always waiting for the other shoe to drop), let people run over them, rarely stand up for themselves, and have generally low self-esteem.

> *Pleaser memories end with the child taking blame—whether or not she was actually at fault.*

If you're an Irish Setter pleaser, you're a sucker for any loser who happens to cross your path. You'll be able to convince yourself that this guy has always been misunderstood, and if someone would just love him, he'd reform himself. Most likely the loser you hook up with is a strong controller, and he'll play you like a Stradivarius. He knows just what buttons to push and how to manipulate your emotions so that you, as a pleaser, will spare no amount of money, time, or energy on him.

> *Learn how to stand up for yourself, how to say no, and how to take charge of your own life.*

One of your greatest weaknesses is basing your sense of self-worth solely on your performance. You need to learn how to stand up for yourself, how to say no, and how to take charge of your own life. You're not important only for what you do—you matter for who you are. But this will be one of the most difficult lessons for you to learn.

The Charmer

You can probably tell by now that Yorkies and lastborns will usually have charmer-related memories. Charmers recall times when they made the entire family laugh or when they manipulated parents, schoolteachers, or siblings to get their way. Memories in which you are the center of attention also qualify as charmer related.

Here's a common charmer memory: "I was five years old, very small for my age, and the last of the grandchildren. One day when we were all gathering at my aunt's house for Thanksgiving, Grandma and Grandpa walked into the dining room, and Grandpa went straight to me, lifted me up, and said, 'Missy, how I've missed you!' He gave me a big kiss and a hug and made me promise that I'd never grow up. Then Grandma said, 'Herbert, don't forget to say hi to the other children. They're waiting for you too.' It made me feel really special that Grandpa paid the most attention to me."

> *Charmers recall times when they made the entire family laugh or when they manipulated parents, schoolteachers, or siblings to get their way.*

If you have charmer memories, you probably enjoy the spotlight. You feel most alive when you've made a room laugh, and you feel most depressed when you think you're being ignored or treated as insignificant. You're probably an extrovert and very likely have a tendency to pout when you don't get your own way.

The important thing to realize is that life won't always go your way.

The Victim

Do your memories leave you feeling like you got a raw deal? Do they dredge up feelings of injustice and perhaps resentment?

If so, you may qualify as a victim.

Victims are frequently middle children. They believe that if something goes wrong, they are the ones most likely to be blamed—because they often have been!

Here's a classic victim memory: "I was six years old. There was a group of about eight children—including two of my siblings—

playing kickball in our front yard. One kid kicked the ball into the road, and a neighbor boy ran out to retrieve it. He didn't look where he was going and ran right in front of a car. The driver slammed on his brakes and missed the kid. We all ran out to the street to see what had happened and were followed closely by my mom. She was so scared and angry, and because I was holding the ball, she assumed I had caused the problem. She spanked me in front of everyone, even though some of the other kids were yelling, 'He didn't do it!' What bugged me most was that she assumed it was me. I was always getting the blame."

> *The important thing to realize is that life won't always go your way.*

As a victim, you consider yourself one of the most unlucky people in the world. You may feel most comfortable when others show you pity. You might be slightly paranoid and eventually develop ailments (such as excessive weight gain or a never-ending list of medical complaints) that fit right in line with how you see yourself. Both of these conditions keep getting you noticed, but eventually you're going to have to learn that's not the best way to be noticed.

Whether you've played the role of the controller, the pleaser, the charmer, or the victim, these roles have shaped your interactions with others. The controller wants respect; the pleaser wants to be appreciated; the charmer wants affection; the victim wants pity. And it's an easy vibe for others to pick up. The nonverbal signals you send clearly mark your rule book.

> *Do your memories leave you feeling like you got a raw deal?*

But is that really who you want to be? Is that how you want people to treat you? If not, it's time to realize how you're coming across—and to make a change.

Confronting the Lies

What would you say if I asked you, "How satisfied are you, really, with where your life is going today?"

Most people would answer with, "Well, it's okay, I guess." Very few of you would say, "Dr. Leman, I gotta tell ya, my life is falling apart."

> What would you say if I asked you, "How satisfied are you, really, with where your life is going today?"

But I know you want *something* to change, or you wouldn't have spent the money to buy this book—or invested the time required to read this far.

If you're already working on the areas you need to change, good for you. I admire you.

But some of you might be like Trisha: "Everything is fine, Dr. Leman. I couldn't be happier. Sure, there have been some tough times, but overall, life has been wonderful."

"Okay," I respond, "so you're comfortable with the fact that you're 31 years old and have had three divorces, one bankruptcy, and a nervous breakdown?"

Or Mac: "You've got it wrong, Dr. Leman. My life is pretty much together. I'm here to help my wife get straightened out, but there's nothing I need."

Lies You Tell Yourself

I'm okay the way I am.
I don't really need to change.
It's not so bad.
I can live with this.

"Oh, really?" I respond. "Well then, can I ask you just one question?"

"Certainly."

"You're 30 years old, and you've already had four careers. Is that by design, or is it a sign that the business world can't be perfect enough for you, that you haven't found your niche?"

People can live lives that show all the marks of chaos, disorganization, and even desperation, but for some reason they maintain an amazing sense of denial, as if nothing has ever been wrong. But if their first and second childhood memories are both negative and their third memory reeks of "You didn't measure up! You're not good enough!" I can tell you these people aren't living a happy life. They feel oppressed, they're striving for something they'll never fully achieve, and they need to be released from the past that binds them. In the present they may say, "Everything's fine!" but memories of their past reveal the truth.

Do you find yourself denying that you need to change—yet something in you longs for change?

Are you in the same boat? Do you find yourself denying that you need to change—yet something in you longs for change?

Think of it this way. You've been the person you are for perhaps 20, 30, or 40 years (or more). You sank into some personality ruts when you were a child, and those ruts were further cemented by your family dynamics during your growing-up years. As a result, you started making assumptions that shaped your rule book.

In short, you've believed the lies you've been telling yourself for a long time. So when you begin to make a change, you'll encounter a lot of internal resistance. Change isn't easy. Rewriting your rule book isn't instant. There's no "fix it" pill that you can take three times a day and then be fine in the morning. But if you determine to reprogram your responses, attitudes, and behaviors, soon the new ones will seem just as normal as the destructive ones used to seem.

Change isn't easy. Rewriting your rule book isn't instant.

Seven Steps to Reprogram Your Rule Book

You were born with a certain disposition that was further cemented and solidified by your birth order and family environment. Consider these factors the "hardware" of your personality.

The "software" took over when things started happening in your life. You were just a little ankle biter, too small even to see over a coffee table, and with virtually no experience. You hadn't traveled to Europe; you weren't educated. No, you were plopped naked into this world, and from that point on, virtually every hour of every day, stimuli started hitting you across the head, and you had to make sense out of all of it: *What gets me noticed? Why do my parents treat me this way? How come my sister gets treated differently?*

You started making assumptions. You started answering the question that would shape your rule book: *I matter only when* _____. You weren't an adult when you made these conclusions. You didn't have a college degree. Your abstract thinking was nil. Still you came up with some definitive answers.

> *Don't hold yourself back. Don't defeat yourself any longer. Determine that you can do it—that you will change.*

The problem is, they may not have been the right ones! Yet you've been stuck in the rut of them.

Now's your chance to use the adult brain God almighty gave you. Don't hold yourself back. Don't defeat yourself any longer. Determine that you can do it—that you *will* change. You *can* be free from fear and all the crap you grew up with. But you have to be willing to take a good, hard look at yourself—where you've been, where you are now, and where you want to go—and make the necessary changes.

If you don't want to be a victim anymore, you don't have to be. It's healthy for you to admit, "You know what? I really have felt most comfortable when people pitied me, but I don't want to be pitied anymore. I want to be respected." That's maturity. That's thinking like a grown-up.

The pleaser may say, "Okay, I grew up thinking I mattered only when I was performing, but that's not true anymore. I want real intimacy based on true relationship. I want to be in a partnership where there is give-and-take." That's called growing up.

So how can you rewrite your rule book?

1. Recognize That the Future Isn't a Prisoner of the Past

Many years ago, I worked with a Vietnamese girl. She was adopted into a very loving and caring American family, but she arrived on our shores with many painful scars—both physical and spiritual. I knew there was a lot of work to do when I inquired about the marks on her arms and she told me they were scars from cigarette burns—one of the worst forms of punishment I've ever come across in decades of counseling. We may never know all that went on in her early childhood.

Not surprisingly, my young client saw the world as a very hateful, hurtful, and spiteful place. Even after living in a warm and protected environment for far longer than she had lived in a horrendous one, she had a very difficult time breaking free from a terrible past. I understood why this was so, but I wasn't about to let her stay there. Yes, she had some awful chapters in her life, but she needed to move on.

You do too. You're an adult now. In order to become the new and healthy "you," you must discard what was done to you and begin to focus on how you want to be treated in the future.

For instance, as a toddler you may have been blamed more often than any of your siblings. You may have felt that you needed to control everything. You may have needed to please others to be accepted.

> *The past has already influenced your present, but how much it influences your future is up to you.*

But you don't have to stay stuck in any of these ruts. You can break out as an adult and say, "That's how I acted in the past. That's what I believed when I was a child. But I'm not a child anymore, and I'm not going to keep acting that way."

You must separate the past from the future. The past has already influenced your present, but how much it influences your future is up to you.

2. Change Your Internal Dialogue

Self-talk is so important here. You can become your own best counselor! My goal with all my clients is always the same: I want them to learn how to counsel themselves so that I'm no longer needed. My job is to give them the basic tools of psychology so they can treat themselves.

Avoid self-defeating talk.

Don't misunderstand me; damaged people need professionals. But even damaged people can eventually learn to take the tools they receive in counseling and strike out on their own. Once you understand your background, your inherent strengths and weaknesses, and the way you've responded to your environment, you can free your future from your past and begin to build on your strengths.

Avoid self-defeating talk. Comments like the following need to be chased out of your vocabulary:

I have no restraint when it comes to food.

I'm always making a mess of things.

I'm the biggest loser in the world.

This type of internal dialogue only further cements the negative bent you received from your childhood.

Here's a better form of internal dialogue:

I've had problems with food in the past, but yesterday was a very good day, and today I've eaten responsibly in two out of three meals, with only one light snack. That's an improvement.

I'm not always good at thinking through a situation before I jump in, but now I stop myself and count to 10 before I act.

In the past, I've failed at a couple of jobs. But now I've picked up some new interpersonal skills, and I really think I can make a go of it this time.

3. Become Your Own Parent

Now that you're an adult, you can talk to yourself like you are your own parent. The difference is that now you have experience. Now you have training. Now you understand how the world works, and out of all that maturity, you can do a better job shaping your own personality.

For instance, the controller can say, "It's scary for me to let others take charge, especially when I'm not sure they can do the job as well as I can. On the other hand, it's arrogant of me to assume that I'm the only one who knows how to do something. This attitude is causing stress in my marriage, negatively imprinting my kids, and giving me a reputation I don't enjoy. It's time to start changing."

Change will come in increments. When the controlling father lets his son wash the car, he is going to have to hold himself back

---

How My Life Changed

When I heard you say on the radio that a kid's personality is pretty much formed by age five, my jaw dropped. My oldest child is about to turn five. He's a sweet kid but an extreme perfectionist. Once he ripped up a note he'd written to his father because one letter wasn't printed well enough for his liking. He can read really well, yet he refuses to do it because he is not as fluent a reader as I am. Whenever he does something wrong, he goes on and on about how much he hates himself for being a bad boy. I've always tried to teach him that making mistakes is all right, and I've tried hard not to let him see my own perfectionistic side, but somehow the message still got through that he had to be perfect.

It took hearing you to realize that before I can change my son, I need to change myself. Easier said than done, I know. But my son is worth it. I just wish I would have realized all this five years ago!

Pat, Ontario

---

from pointing out every little spot that Junior missed. No, Junior probably can't wash the car as well as Dad can, but so what? Are you entering your vehicle in some sort of spotless-car contest?

Build yourself up with well-deserved encouragement. Be gentle with yourself when you fail.

So why not talk to yourself like a good authoritative parent talks to his or her children? Build yourself up with well-deserved encouragement. Be gentle with yourself when you fail. Learn to judge your behavior objectively and to correct it accordingly.

Don't just act and don't just feel—think! Examine why you feel comfortable always being in control, why you're always trying to please someone, why you crave the limelight so much, or why your first instinct is to seek someone's pity—then remind yourself why you don't want to play that role anymore.

4. Make a Bad Memory Good

When actor Jack Lemmon died in 2001, an article recounting his life caught my eye because one story in it was so similar to my own. Remember when I messed up a cheer as a little kid and made everyone laugh? Lemmon did the same thing, only it was in a play and not a cheer. He was eight years old, and because another kid got sick, Jack was asked to step in and help out with a school play. Jack got his first line right but messed up on the second one. His classmates started to laugh. What could have been a humiliating experience became a liberating one, however. Instead of fighting it, crying, or running away in embarrassment, Lemmon started milking the mistake for even more laughs. By the time he was done, the entire class applauded![11]

Looking back, Jack saw that incident as a turning point in his life. "I thought to myself, 'I think I like this.' This was the greatest day of my life."[12]

For many kids, getting laughed at by an entire class would be a humiliating day at best, but for Jack it was the start of something special. He had discovered his calling and used this gift to make the most of his career, ultimately appearing in more than five hundred TV shows and acting in some hilarious movies with one of his favorite sidekicks, Walter Matthau. They don't make comedies much better than *Grumpy Old Men*. Along the way, Lemmon won two Oscars and an Emmy.

There isn't a single person alive who doesn't harbor some bad and even painful memories. Consider one woman who as a child experienced rape and poverty. Then she finally got a job at a local television station but was told by that same station that her nose, her hair, and her mouth were "all wrong." She went to a French hairdresser in New York City to try to do something about her hair and ended up going bald and getting scabs on her scalp!

Still she persisted, finally getting a chance to appear on Joan Rivers's show, where Rivers humiliated her by asking her why she was so fat. The fact that she could hear her own thighs rub together was enough to convince her to go to a fat farm to lose weight, but the visit was cut short when Steven Spielberg called to say he thought she would be perfect for the part of Sofia in a new movie he was filming called *The Color Purple*. The offer came with a warning, however. He said that if she lost one more pound, he might have to give the role to a different actress. Oprah Winfrey left the fat farm that day, stopping at a Dairy Queen on the way home.[13]

Successful people usually have as many bad memories as "regular" people do. In fact, they often have more. When a reporter

> *Successful people usually have as many bad memories as "regular" people do. The difference is that successful people use their bad memories as motivation to create good memories.*

asked Ernest Hemingway how to become a good writer, he responded, "Have a lousy childhood."

The difference is that successful people use their bad memories as motivation to create good memories. Jack Lemmon found something positive in making others laugh—even at his expense—and used it to become a famous actor. Oprah fought her way out of poverty and stereotyping to become America's favorite big sister.

> *The only power that memories have to hold you back is the power you give them.*

Here's a secret you need to learn: the only power that memories have to hold you back is the power you give them. Don't run from your memories. Remember them! Cultivate them, reevaluate them, and then use them as motivation. Find out the positive side of each hurtful one. Even if something was truly terrible, such as Oprah's rape, you can think, *That was awful, but I survived.* Even bad memories, looked at through this lens, can make us stronger.

For instance, let's take the situation my Vietnamese client faced. Instead of saying, "I was burned as a baby; therefore the world is an awful place," she could say, "What was done to me was terrible. No baby should have to go through that. But I landed on my feet. God placed me in a loving family. Things changed, and there's no reason to believe they won't keep changing for the better."

A boy who missed an easy word at a spelling bee and was laughed at mercilessly can comfort himself by saying, "You know what? The pressure was on, I got nervous, and I missed an easy word. It can happen to anyone. My worth isn't tied up in the fact that, as a second grader, I couldn't spell 'mitt.' It's time to move on."

The boy we mentioned earlier who was spanked in front of his friends could revisit his memories and say, "I bet Mom was really scared. And while it wasn't fair of her to blame me, and while it's true that I often got blamed for things I didn't do, I don't live with

---

How My Life Changed

I spent 20 years being mad at my dad for the way he treated me when I was a kid. A month ago, Dad died. That next week, after hearing you talk on a radio show, it hit me: I would never have a relationship with my dad. And I'd just realized why my dad had done some of the things he'd done—because that's the way he was parented too. Worse, I saw some of the same things in myself (I'm a dad now too). It's too late for me and Dad, but it's not too late for me and my son, Justin.

Tate, Michigan

---

my mom anymore. When I go to work, they don't see me as the middle child; they see me as the accounts manager. I do good work, and my fear of failing is irrational. I haven't gotten a bad evaluation yet. In fact, my boss has been talking about a promotion and raise. I've really grown in my competence as a worker, and now it's time to grow emotionally as a person."

5. Forgive Your Parents

Our culture has made parent bashing a national sport. Rather than take responsibility for who we have become, we like to pawn off the blame on dysfunctional Dad and maniacal Mom.

Admittedly, as a counselor I've seen more than my share of parental horror stories. I know how cruel, vindictive, and downright hurtful some parents can be, but what I'm about to say is based on my experience working with children from very dysfunctional families: the worse your home life was, the more you need to forgive your parents.

The worse your home life was, the more you need to forgive your parents.

Some of you have it backwards. You think that if your parents were average or maybe even slightly below average, you could forgive them. But if they're the bottom 10 percent, you could never forgive them.

I think it's just the opposite, because I believe forgiveness is one of the best tools you can use for emotional self-defense. When you have a chance, check out Dr. Lewis Smedes's groundbreaking book *Forgive and Forget*, and you'll find out that the first person served by forgiveness is the person who does the forgiving!

Bitterness, prolonged anger, and resentment are emotional toxins; they poison our souls. Forgiveness is the great cauterizer. It burns away diseased emotions and frees us from the prison of the past.

I know what I'm talking about here. Neighbor kids used to call the gin mill my dad's office. I come from a long line of drinkers, and I've had my share of forgiving to do. I've learned that I will gain nothing and lose quite a bit if I hold on to the past and remain bitter and angry and spiteful.

> You need to forgive—not because your parents deserve forgiveness, but because you deserve the freedom that comes from the act of forgiving.

When I encourage you to remember your early childhood memories, I want you to reject the lies that have shaped your private logic and have written your rule book. You need to forgive—not because your parents deserve forgiveness, but because *you* deserve the freedom that comes from the act of forgiving.

Perhaps you had good parents who occasionally messed up. Many parents don't need forgiveness as much as they need understanding. No one is perfect, and it's guaranteed that someone you live with for 18 years or more will occasionally let you down or say something unkind. Don't resent your parents because they're human. Understanding their weaknesses can go a long way to clarifying your relationship.

If your parents are still alive, initiate forgiveness by getting together with them. Stress that you'd like to get to know them all over again—as an adult—if that relationship can be based on mutual respect. In some cases, however (such as the case of abuse), personal contact is best avoided. But that doesn't mean your own heart can't move toward forgiveness.

6. Take Action

Change is nothing more than an empty word unless you make the effort to put the insights you've learned to good use.

For example, a woman who has a habit of getting into destructive romantic relationships can say, "I'm not going to have sex anymore until I get married. I have to make a change so I can find someone who truly cares about me, not just someone who is looking out for his own pleasure."

The man who can't hold down a job can say, "The next time I get angry at my boss or the next time I'm told to do something I think is stupid, I'm not going to quit. I've left too many good-paying jobs in the heat of the moment. From now on, the only way I'll leave a place of employment is through a written letter of resignation, giving me a chance to really think about my decision instead of just acting on emotion."

Real change won't take place until you confront the lies, change your rule book to think these thoughts, and then put them into action.

7. Partner with Someone

If you truly want to change, tell someone you trust about it and ask for help: "Megan, I'm trying to shake Krispy Kremes. When we go out to have coffee, could you help remind me?"

When you're accountable to no one, you risk drifting with no port of call in sight. The drift might be slow, but a steady drift can take you a long way if it's not stopped. You can begin change right now by picking up the telephone, telling someone you want to change, and enlisting his or her help. Public confession shows both you and others that you honestly mean business.

Don't Believe the Lies!

Zane Grey was told he couldn't write. Thomas Edison was not thought to be very bright. And Albert Einstein? Well, he was a brick short of a full load.

Now, I ask you, what would have happened if those three brilliant people had believed the lies—and internalized them?

Trying to change yourself is much harder than trying to change someone else. Could that be because of the lies you tell yourself *about* yourself? That you're not worth it? That you're not good enough? That you can't do it because you tried before and failed? That it's all your parents' fault for the way they raised you?

Now's the time to expose the lies—for your own good and for those you love. Why not step up to the plate and become the person you've always longed to be?

I know you're smart, so why not play the game of life smart?

What to Do on Wednesday

1. Look back at your list of three early childhood memories. How do they influence your current private logic?
2. Make a list of what's in your rule book. How has this rule book helped you become who you want to be? Hindered you from becoming a new you?
3. Identify your parents' style of child rearing:
   - Authoritarian
   - Permissive
   - Critical
   - Authoritative
4. Pinpoint which of these you tend to be:
   - Controller
   - Pleaser
   - Charmer
   - Victim
5. Reread the section "Seven Steps to Reprogram Your Rule Book."

Thursday

How Do You Spell "Love"?
(My Wife Spells it V-i-s-a)

What makes you feel loved, and what does that say about you?
Understanding your own style and the styles of others can
smooth relational road bumps.

Just before Sande's and my fifteenth wedding anniversary, I was
walking around a store, thinking about what I should buy for her
to surprise her, when I came across the perfect present. There, on
the shelf in front of me, sat the sleekest, most durable, and most
beautiful toaster you have ever seen in your entire life. And it was
a four-slicer! None of those puny two-slice toasters for *my* wife.
I wanted her to have the very best to show her how much I love
her. And this gourmet appliance even had wide enough slots to
toast bagels. What more could Sande ask for?

I bought the toaster and had the lady at the store wrap it up.
"Is this a wedding present?" she asked.

"No," I said, "it's an anniversary present for my wife."

Much to my surprise, the nice lady kept shooting dirty glances my way. I assumed she was thinking about her own husband, wondering why he didn't have the good sense to get her such a fine gift. She must have been thinking, *Why couldn't I have had the good fortune to marry such a sensitive, creative man?*

Yeah, that had to be it.

A few hours later, it was that magical moment: Sande opened the present I had so thoughtfully chosen for her. "Oh, how nice," she said—and put it in a prominent place in the kitchen.

I felt all warm inside, knowing I had hit a home run.

Half an hour later, I noticed I hadn't seen Sande in a while. Well, to be honest, it was my then five-year-old son, Kevin, who gave me the clue.

"Dad," he asked, "why is Mommy crying in the bathroom with the door closed?"

I groaned, knowing I had made a mistake—a big one—again. I thought I'd learned.

> *This gourmet appliance even had wide enough slots to toast bagels. What more could Sande ask for?*

You see, early on in our marriage, I used to buy Sande underwear that she would never wear. She claimed, of all ridiculous things, that the kind I bought was "too uncomfortable." It took me a few years to discover that Sande's idea of comfortable panties bears a startling resemblance to maternity underwear. She thinks there needs to be room for two, even though she's a very slender woman.

Then there was the time I thought I should work more on romancing my wife, so I went to the department store and got Sande this knockout nightie. Man, was it hot. Sande opened the gift, remarked how pretty it was, kissed me on the cheek, and put it back in the box. That was the last time I saw that nightie until two years later, when I dug it up from the bottom of a ragbag with the faint aroma of lemon Pledge on it. To my knowledge, that nightie became the most expensive dust rag in the history of the world.

My gift-giving history (which has improved, by the way, giving the rest of the romantic putzes of the world some hope) is good proof of how most of us act in relationships. We give others what we really want. But what about what the other person wants?

Sometimes the best present you can give someone is to find something nearly identical to what they most recently gave you.

You'll do yourself a major favor by understanding that different people want to be loved in different ways and through different means. What excites you and is meaningful to you may not be meaningful to others. Having this understanding will help you further define your own unique qualities as well as help you explain yourself to others. It will also help you learn how to love people who are special to you in a way that produces more intimate relationships.

Learning to love doesn't come naturally to any of us; it's a skill we need to learn. Fortunately, there's help. My friend Gary Chapman has written a wonderful book, *The Five Love Languages*, that helps to identify every person's emotional needs. His book

> *Sometimes the best present you can give someone is to find something nearly identical to what they most recently gave you.*

> *Learning to love doesn't come naturally to any of us; it's a skill we need to learn.*

Lies You Tell Yourself

I like it, so she'll like it.
Of course, *everyone* wants one of those. Who wouldn't?
There's only one way to express love to your spouse: sex.
He ought to be able to figure out what I like. I shouldn't have to tell him!

is written particularly for married couples, but it's also intriguing for those who are thinking of dating or are involved in a dating relationship.

What Fills Your Tank?

Did you know that it is rare for a husband and wife to share the same love language? That means the wife will often love her husband just how *she* wants to be loved—and leave her husband's emotional love tank empty as a result. The frustrated husband will in turn love his wife just how *he* wants to be loved, hoping she'll get the hint. Of course, she doesn't, because she can't imagine why her husband is treating her the way he is. She doesn't want to be loved like that, so there's no way she's going to love her husband that way.

That's how the emotional distance in marriage can begin growing.

I'll be blunt. Behind every failed marriage, rebellious kid, or broken relationship is an empty love tank. Deep down, that person is not feeling loved because he or she isn't receiving the specific kind of attention that says "I love you." I remember one client who came to see me, exhausted by the emotional distance in her marriage. Both she and her husband worked all the time, and I remember thinking, *This woman is a prime candidate for marital infidelity. And so is her husband.*

"Have you been tempted to have an affair?" I asked her.

She almost laughed. "Already been there and done that," she confessed. "How'd you know?"

It's not rocket science. An empty love tank is often a contributing factor for marital breakdown—and also juvenile delinquency. If you want to have a successful, happy life and a healthy home, and you want to be the "new you" you dream of becoming, it's vital that you are able to identify your own love language and learn to speak your loved one's as well.

Love Language #1: Words of Affirmation

Silence is never golden for people whose love language is words of affirmation. There are certain members of the human race who live for an aptly spoken compliment, a tender endearment, or a word of encouragement. You can do all sorts of positive things for these individuals—make them a nice meal, give them a hearty hug, spend long hours in their presence—but if you don't verbalize your affection and commitment, they won't feel loved.

I call words of affirmation "slipping your loved ones commercial messages." In my practice, for instance, I've heard more than my share of negative, critical parenting, and I've witnessed firsthand the devastating destruction that harsh parenting can do. Perhaps because of this experience, I go out of my way to provide encouraging commentaries that build up my kids: "Honey, taking you and your friends home from the ice-skating rink reminded me of what a good job you've done choosing your friends; they're wonderful girls, every one of them, and I'm proud of the decisions you've made."

> *There are certain members of the human race who live for an aptly spoken compliment, a tender endearment, or a word of encouragement.*

So if your loved one has that love language, why not use it? Let's say your son has been struggling with his golf swing and finally gets a hit. Why not simply say, "Well, Tommy, it looks like that practice is really paying off!"

My friend Moonhead and I were in a restaurant once when we saw a guy wearing a shirt that made me chuckle. Since I used to play golf, I could relate. The shirt had four lines:

"I hate golf."

"I hate golf."

"Nice shot, buddy."

"I love golf."

Amazing how one positive phrase can completely transform a frustrating ordeal, isn't it?

But I'm not talking about empty praise—that false, sickeningly sweet stuff—either. Meaningful encouragement is noticing a positive trait in a child or spouse or friend and saying, "That's a trait to hold on to and build upon."

This love language often produces the most trouble in a marriage when it's a love language favored by the wife, in large part because men aren't that good with words. We're great with noises, grunts, and commands, but terms of endearment? Let's just say, in general, men could do a whole lot better. On average, men use three times fewer words per day than women. By the time most of us men get home from work, 99 percent of our words are used up. I've never had a man tell me that, after coming home from a long day at the office, his first thought was, *What I could really use is a good 45-minute talk with my wife.* Such a man may exist, but I haven't met him yet! Given this, it's not difficult to see how women who feel loved primarily through words of affirmation might feel shortchanged in many marriages.

> *I've never had a man tell me that, after coming home from a long day at the office, his first thought was,* What I could really use is a good 45-minute talk with my wife.

If you're a man reading this, may I suggest that you need to reconsider your silence out of love for your wife and kids? I've counseled a surprising number of men who told me, "Look, Dr.

Leman, I made a promise to my wife on our wedding day, and I intend to keep it."

"What was your promise?"

"I told her that I loved her very much and that if things ever changed, she'd be the first to know. In the meantime, unless I bring it up again, she doesn't need to worry about whether I love her. She can remember what I told her on our wedding day."

Sorry, buddy, but that's not gonna cut it if your wife's love language is words of affirmation. She needs to hear it again and again and again.

Your marriage isn't like an old-growth forest; it's like a newly planted garden. Old-growth forests are pretty sturdy. They don't need to be watered. They don't need to be weeded. If we don't pollute them, poison them, or burn them down, they're going to do just fine.

> *Your marriage isn't like an old-growth forest; it's like a newly planted garden.*

A garden, on the other hand, is the exact opposite. If you don't water it, if you don't make sure it gets enough sunlight, if you don't weed it and care for it and fertilize it, you won't get squat. You'll have a salad with one puny carrot and a bug-infested head of lettuce.

Your marriage is like that garden. One watering won't last for 50 years. You need to water your marriage every day, sometimes every hour.

So, men, if words of affirmation is your wife's love language, let me help you apply this advice. Your wife needs for you to take some words and do something that might not seem natural to you. Think of it as a building project, only this time you're going to build a

> *A sentence requires several things, including a subject, a verb, and an object. "Huh?" "What?" "I dunno," and "Whatever" do not qualify as sentences.*

sentence. A sentence requires several things, including a subject, a verb, and an object. "Huh?" "What?" "I dunno," and "Whatever" do not qualify as sentences for this discussion. The sentences I'm talking about go like this:

> "I love you more today than I ever have. Life with you just keeps getting sweeter."
>
> "You're so good to me. How could I ever make it without you?"
>
> "I was feeling a little down today, so I just started thinking about you. That made me feel a whole lot better."

Any one of the above statements can be uttered in ten seconds or less, but each one can be a highlight of your wife's week if the words are said with sincerity.

For those men who have a hard time expressing themselves, I suggest you use a word picture. Men often aren't very good with feelings, so we can do better with images: "I'm so angry I feel like a dog trying to tear apart a raw steak." "I feel like the weight of the world has been put on my shoulders, and I'm too tired to keep standing up." "At work I feel like I have two strikes against me and an umpire who hates me; there's no way I can avoid striking out."

I know some of you may feel uncomfortable talking about fears, emotions, or dreams, but that's okay. You want to be a new you, right? Becoming a new you is sometimes uncomfortable. It means changing the way you relate to others—starting with the ones closest to you. It means stepping out on a limb to make your spouse (and children, if you have any) feel loved, cherished, and fulfilled.

If your spouse's love language is words of affirmation, drop all negatives. Complaining and nagging won't do a thing for you. With those who have a verbal love language, positive words rev them up like nothing else—but negative comments bring them as low as they can get. They are extremely sensitive to both praise and criticism. Criticism will just shut them down.

If you want to really make your spouse smile, spread good gossip about him or her to others. I guarantee it'll get back to your spouse.

If your love language is verbal and you're single, find a man or woman who knows how to communicate verbally. If you're married to a person whose love language is verbal, you simply have to develop the skills of conversation; that's the only way your spouse will feel loved.

Love Language #2: Quality Time

I had a mom come to me who was frustrated about her relationship with her oldest daughter. She went out of her way to verbally engage her daughter but seemed to get nowhere. Her husband, on the other hand, was the silent, brooding type who rarely spoke, but he had their daughter's undying devotion and affection.

Mom just couldn't understand how this quiet man could have captured his daughter's heart when she, who peppered her daughter with questions, seemed to get nowhere.

I spent some time talking to the daughter and immediately picked up on the problem. When the parents and I got back together, I asked the mom a couple simple questions, beginning with, "When your daughter has a hard time getting to sleep, what CD does she like to listen to?"

"I don't know."

"New Kids on the Block," Dad answered.

"Right," I said.

"How did you know that, dear?" Mom asked her husband.

"Because sometimes she asks me to put it on when I leave the room."

I continued. "When your daughter is at the plate while playing softball, what does she do?"

Mom looked dumbfounded.

"She hits the plate twice with the bat when she's feeling confident, but she looks back at me when she's feeling nervous," Dad said.

This daughter's love language was quality time. Dad gave her that time, whereas Mom gave her only words. And the questions Mom peppered her with didn't feel like affirmation; they felt like the grand inquisition. By and large, adolescents don't like questions. Given this, it was only natural that the daughter felt closer to her dad. He loved her the way she wanted to be loved.

> It was only natural that the daughter felt closer to her dad. He loved her the way she wanted to be loved.

One of the best ways for me to show love to one of my daughters as she was growing up was to sit down and listen to her new CDs. I happened to be a Dixie Chicks fan, so it didn't take much sacrifice to listen to their latest CD, but love for my daughter was the *only* reason I've ever sat down to hear *NSYNC and the Backstreet Boys croon their way to another bestselling CD. And when she came up with something I didn't like? As long as it didn't have offensive lyrics, I'd find one positive thing about it and mention that: "Well, it's got a good beat," or, "That woman has a knockout voice."

Some spouses and kids couldn't care less about receiving gifts. They want your time. They want you to sit with them, take walks with them, go to ball games with them, watch a movie with them, or just get home in time to eat dinner with them. It doesn't cost you money to do this. They aren't necessarily asking to spend time at the beach, a resort, or a palace—they just want you by their side.

Kids who have this love language want you at their games. It's not the same if you get too busy, miss the game, and then offer to sit down and listen to a recap. They want to look up in the stands and see you there. If they're singing in the choir, they don't care if you can't make out their voices. Their love tank feels full when they catch sight of your familiar face as they look out into the audience.

Sande really touched my heart a few years into our marriage when she showed up to watch me receive my doctorate degree. That may not sound like much to you, but consider the circumstances: I received my degree on a Saturday afternoon, and on Thursday night (about 36 hours previously), Sande had given birth to our second daughter, Krissy. Sande was still in a wheelchair, but she made it to the ceremony, and it meant so much to me that she gave such a heroic effort to watch me get my doctorate.

> *Some spouses and kids couldn't care less about receiving gifts. They want your time.*

If your spouse or kids have quality time as their primary love language, you must get ruthless with your schedule. If you don't draw up some guidelines, overinvolvement will wreck your family.

I have a great little exercise to help overinvolved families. Right off the bat, I'll tell them to list everything everyone is involved in. The list can become almost humorous if the consequences weren't so dire. I've seen some boys play on three different baseball teams—during the same season. I've had dads off golfing while mom is riding horses and the kids are farmed out all over the city.

Once the list is laid in front of me, I give them a marker and say, "All right, cut out half of it."

"You've got to be kidding!" they'll protest.

"I'm not. You must cut down your activities by 50 percent."

Some of these families are like alcoholics—they're so busy they truly don't understand the stress behind what they're doing. They can get desperate when they're finally urged to make some choices and to realize that sometimes you have to pass up even some very profitable activities to avoid becoming too busy.

Once the painful cuts are made, my next advice is to get them to write a little saying on a note card and put it by the phone. The saying goes like this: "If there's any doubt, say no." Too-busy people have faulty filters. In the back of their minds, they get little warnings like, "Does Susan really have time to do one more activity?" but then the mom starts rationalizing and thinking about what her daughter will "miss out on," and before you know it, the already tired kid has just been signed up for her tenth weekly commitment. In my book, if there's any doubt at all, respond by cutting it out. Unless you can absolutely defend spending time on this activity, get rid of it.

If there's any doubt, say no.

I don't mean this to sound like a warning, but in many ways it really is: if you don't spend quality time with people who have this love language, they won't feel loved, and we live in a day and age in which many waiting arms are available for neglected people. In case I'm not being specific enough, I'll be more direct: your loved ones will eventually find someone who wants to spend time with them. If it's not you, they'll hook up with someone else. Your teenage son will find a young girl and maybe get her pregnant, or he'll start hanging out with a drug-dealing gang of guys if his family is too busy to create a sense of belonging. The person who truly stands alone is one in a trillion. Almost all of us keep looking until we find someone who wants to be in our presence.

Almost all of us keep looking until we find someone who wants to be in our presence.

For the person who feels loved by quality time, quantity can't be ignored either. Quality time won't make up for a lack of quantity; kids just don't think that way. However, in the midst of providing a generous quantity of time, don't also forget to carve out *meaningful* time. Watching TV together may boost CBS's ratings, but it won't mean squat to your kid or spouse. Reading a newspaper at the breakfast table puts the two of you in the same room but on entirely different planets. Having the radio on while you're in the car together doesn't create any communal memories.

Meaningful time doesn't happen by accident; you have to choose it. You're going to have to motivate yourself to turn off the television, go outside, and shoot baskets with your son. Instead of running off by yourself, maybe you can shock the family by suggesting you all get together and play Yahtzee or Monopoly. Or perhaps you can tell the kids to finish up the dishes and then take your wife by the hand, telling her, "Come on, honey, let's go for a walk. I want to hear about your day."

> *Watching TV together may boost CBS's ratings, but it won't mean squat to your kid or spouse.*

You'll also want to focus on occasional quality events. If your husband is a big baseball fan, maybe you could buy two tickets to a game and surprise him, even if nine innings sounds eight innings too long. If your daughter loves jazz dance, take her to a performance, even if you think dancing is boring. If your wife is a big fan of art and you hear about the local museum getting a new exhibition, mention it to her. It will mean so much more to your loved one that you were the initiator, rather than reluctantly responding to his or her request.

> *Meaningful time doesn't happen by accident; you have to choose it.*

Don't Just Spend Time—Make a Memory

Look into your spouse's eyes.
Give her your full attention.
Keep your mouth shut until she finishes talking. (Very hard for us men, since we immediately want to problem solve.)
Watch her body language.
Listen for what's going on in her heart.

How My Life Changed

My wife and I always got along okay, but two months ago we hit an all-time low. Our marriage was boring, we both finally agreed. So in May we attended a marriage seminar of yours. Life will never be the same (and thank God it won't!).

We are both middleborn children (no wonder there was no passion in our marriage and we both sat around like couch potatoes on Friday night), but we had no clue how the traits of middleborns had affected our marriage. I also had no idea how important it was to my wife to receive gifts (her love language). Guess I'd forgotten about that a couple years into our marriage. Every day now I try to come up with a little thing I can give my wife—even if it's a daisy from our backyard on her pillow—to tell her I love her. All I can say is . . . Friday nights are no longer boring. In fact, sometimes we have to send the kids to Grandma's for the night.

Sean, Tennessee

Love Language #3: Receiving Gifts

All right, you already know gift giving isn't my forte, but in my defense, my wife isn't exactly the easiest person to buy gifts for. She used to have her own store called the Shabby Hattie, where she sold things affectionately known as "shabby chic." Leman translation: Stuff people used to throw away but now pay top dollar to acquire.

When she had that store, I was really in trouble. You see, what she liked the most, she bought and put in her store. But I couldn't buy presents *for* my wife *from* my wife. She wouldn't give me credit!

Once when we were summering in upstate New York, Sande came across some old beat-up fence boards. Naturally she thought someone would love to pay a good bit of money for these old boards and use them to decorate, so she stored them outside until she could take them back to Tucson. The boards couldn't get any more beat-up than they already were, so there was no need to cover them.

About the same time, we had a rather intriguing man—let's just say he was a colorful man with a colorful vocabulary—come to clean out our septic tank. I'm not sure what made up this guy's history, but any man with just seven fingers certainly has a few stories to tell.

He drove into our yard, started cleaning out the septic tank, and then found that his truck was full and needed to be emptied before he could finish the job. He didn't want to leave the septic tank open, so he looked around our yard to see if there were any worthless objects that he could use to cover the hole.

Guess what he found?

Tastes differ, but what we give and how we receive gifts say an awful lot about us. The best gift Sande ever gave me, besides my prized jukebox, was one she had made. She took the cover from my very first book, framed it, and put a gold plate on the bottom that read, "Number one husband, number one father, number one author." The whole thing couldn't have cost her more than $20, but to me it's priceless, because that gift told me Sande knew me, knew my heart. And she was thinking of me and what would mean the most to me.

If you are married to someone whose love language is receiving gifts, you need to get creative, within your budget, at finding gifts. A gift need not cost a hundred bucks or more. A good gift might be a flower, a prized baseball card, tickets to a game or the opera. . . . Just think about your spouse. What would he or she like? The gift could be free or costly, but it needs to be a gift.

> *What we give and how we receive gifts say an awful lot about us.*

> *If you are married to someone whose love language is receiving gifts, you need to get creative, within your budget, at finding gifts.*

Women, you might think that doing everything at home (the laundry, the cooking, the bill paying, and then some) is enough. But if your husband is a gift receiver and you don't give him gifts that are specially suited to him, he'll feel slighted.

If you're single and you like to receive gifts, don't marry a self-obsessed man or a man with little creativity. Here's a clue, by the way: however creative he is while dating, divide that creativity in half, and that's what you can expect in marriage. If you're already disappointed with this guy while you're still single, don't even think about marrying him. Dump the chump. He won't improve, regardless of what he says.

> *However creative he is while dating, divide that creativity in half, and that's what you can expect in marriage.*

Men, you might think that providing an income such that your wife can choose to work or not, having a spacious home, and buying late-model vehicles for your wife speaks for itself in regard to your affection. But if your wife's love language is receiving gifts, she'll feel nothing but emotional distance in that new house and new car. So fill both of them up with visual symbols of your love.

To show a woman this kind of love, you need to get to know her. For starters, you need to understand her well enough to know if she would think something is tacky or endearing. Is she motivated by the price and place of purchase or by the thought behind it? Does she care if you remember that yellow roses are her favorite, or is she happy to get *any* flowers because the mere act of giving something shows you were thinking about her?

When my son, Kevin, was just four years old, he absolutely melted Sande's heart, even though his act was blatant thievery. He woke up one morning, took a tour of the neighborhood, and helped himself to our fellow residents' most colorful flowers. He then walked into the kitchen and handed his mommy a precious bouquet. Sande was purring for hours (though I noticed she put

> ### How My Life Changed
>
> I love my husband, but he's a real dud when it comes to gift giving. He is a great provider, always helps with the kids, and is an easy guy to get along with. Life should be wonderful, huh? I've always felt empty, though, on days like Valentine's Day and our anniversary. I never realized why until I found out, in your seminar last week, that my love language is receiving gifts. I think the last gift I got from my husband was my engagement ring. I also remembered what you said about men being dumber than mud sometimes about things women like. So I talked to Dave about it.
>
> The look on his face was priceless! It was that dumber-than-mud stare you said I'd get. But when I told him how important it was to me to receive gifts, he got it. And he's really trying. In the week since I was at the seminar, he's brought me a red rose (hey, I'd have been thrilled even with the daisies in the backyard), a candy bar I love, and a surprise dinner bag of all my favorite foods. You were right. I shouldn't have judged the guy for what he had no clue about. He just needed a little nudging. Well, so did I. Thanks for being the nudger.
>
> Sandra, Nebraska

the flowers in a place where they couldn't be seen through the windows).

Just as thoughtful gifts can work wonders, so wrongheaded gifts can hurt people deeply. When a dad buys his 16-year-old daughter an age-inappropriate gift—getting her a Mary Kate and Ashley DVD, for instance, just because she liked the twins as a preadolescent—his daughter feels misunderstood, insulted, and unloved. To truly give a gift well, the gift must be given out of understanding and intimacy.

And here's the kicker: sometimes love requires us to *receive* a gift rather than just give a gift. Some people are martyr types—always doing things for others. But they never allow anyone to do anything for them. While this seems generous, they are actually denying others the pleasure they receive from giving.

If your spouse, friend, or family member likes to give gifts, learn how to receive them—for their sake, not yours. You might indeed use the nightie as a dust rag or the ghastly tie as something with which to wipe off your car's oil dipstick, but be gracious. Receiving gifts can be just as important as giving gifts.

Love Language #4: Acts of Service

I have a friend who travels a good bit and whose wife hates the thought of going to gas stations. It's like she's allergic to them. She'll drive a car on fumes for six months before she'll go through a self-serve line. Before most of my friend's trips, one of his last acts is to check the gas gauge on the family minivan. If it's below half a tank, he makes sure he fills it up.

What he may not realize is that he's filling more than a gas tank—he's also filling his wife's love tank. Some people respond best to concrete acts of service. Even things like changing the cat's litter box or scooping up dog droppings in the backyard can seem almost romantic to the person for whom it is done.

If you're a woman and your love language is acts of service, you probably feel most loved when your husband or boyfriend fixes your plumbing, changes the oil in your car, or helps you put together something you bought from Costco.

If you're a man, you may feel most loved when your wife or girlfriend bakes you special treats or saves you the hassle of shopping for clothes by picking up something for you to wear.

I have another friend who is more of the literary sort. He majored in English at college, likes words, and even used to write poetry. He has tried to love his wife with words of affirmation, using creative phrases rather than stock clichés, and one time his wife responded, "Oh, good one, Jim!" Anna admired his creativity, but it didn't really touch her heart.

He also tried buying her creative gifts, such as a Japanese buckwheat pillow and special health food treats. Anna appreciates them, but they don't overwhelm her, even when he guesses correctly on something she would truly enjoy.

What she really likes is when her husband does what he hates: replacing a leaking toilet, fixing a broken hinge, hanging up a heavy mirror.

When they moved into a new house, Anna bought a living room mirror that weighed about 60 pounds. Jim was afraid to hang it because he knew if he did, it would eventually fall down and break. That mirror sat against the wall of the living room for three months, and every day that it stayed there Anna felt a little more frustrated and a little less loved. She didn't want words. She didn't want any gifts. She wanted the stupid mirror hung.

When Jim finally broke down and got a friend to help him do it right, Anna rewarded him that night in a very intimate and creative way. But here's what's even more interesting: Jim and Anna had been married for five years until he finally began to realize what really makes his wife feel loved—and what makes her want to love him back! For some of you, it's been a lot longer than that.

People who love acts of service tend to be less sentimental and far more practical than the words or gifts crowd. All that romance is fine for an occasional diversion, but the bread and butter on which they want to exist consists of doing practical things that make their lives easier.

I know I'm going to sound repetitious here, but again, I want singles to consider this as part of the dating experience. Women, if you know this is your love language

> *What she really likes is when her husband does what he hates: replacing a leaking toilet, fixing a broken hinge, hanging up a heavy mirror.*

> *People who love acts of service tend to be less sentimental and far more practical than the words or gifts crowd.*

and you plan to marry a guy who got a doctorate degree in early American literature but who couldn't put together a 12-piece puzzle, much less a desk from Costco, think twice.

If you're a single man with this love language, don't marry a lazy, ditzy woman. Marry someone who has the initiative and ability that is so important to you.

Love Language #5: Physical Touch

I once had a client who was probably better fed than any husband I've ever met. His wife loves to cook, and when I say "cook," I don't mean heat up some store-bought lasagna. She's one of those who thinks presentation is as important as taste, so she plans dinners not just by their taste and nutritional content but by how the various colors will look on the plate.

She's Martha Stewart's twin. Her husband's closet is so organized it gives me a headache just looking at it. Every shoe has its place, and virtually every sock and piece of underwear has been inventoried and cataloged.

He never forgets one of his relative's birthdays or anniversaries, because his Martha Stewart wife reminds him precisely three weeks before each event. If he hasn't done anything with that information, she gives him a reminder at two weeks. If he tarries another day or two, she presents him with three card options and asks him to sign one.

I don't know that any man has ever been taken care of quite so well. Even so, he ended up in my office, frustrated at the tremendous lack of love he felt in his marriage. His wife couldn't understand his sense of alienation. What more could she do for him? She was already doing it all.

I'll tell you what I told her. She could touch him. Anywhere, at any time, and at virtually any place. He wanted physical affection. Without that touch, he would never feel loved.

Gary Chapman writes, "Physical touch can make or break a relationship. It can communicate love or hate. To the person whose primary love language is physical touch, the message will be far more than the words 'I hate you' or 'I love you.' A slap in the face is detrimental to any child, but it is devastating to a child whose primary love language is touch. A tender hug communicates love to any child. But it shouts love to the child whose primary love language is physical touch. The same is true of adults."[1]

There's an incredible power in touching for both sexes. Many women love to be touched (note to you men: touched and stroked, not grabbed). Men aren't that much different. For 90 percent of us, if you want to get our attention, just touch us. You can touch us anywhere—any part of the body is good! (Okay, some places are more special than others.)

When women ask me how they can get their men to listen to them, I usually encourage them to use touch before and while they talk. That gets hubby's (or boyfriend's) attention. Kiss the back of his neck, put your arm inside his, gently nibble at his ear. He's all yours. Then, as you're touching him, you can slip him the commercial announcement you want him to hear.

Try it and see. For most men, this approach works far better than buying your husband a Miracle-Ear. Plus it's a lot cheaper and you won't have to keep batteries around the house.

A touch is powerful. At my dad's funeral, Bill Foster, one of my best friends, never said a word to me. He just walked up to me and touched my arm. That's all he had to do. I knew exactly how he felt and exactly what he was saying.

This is an area where a woman can completely miss her husband's heart. A wife does so many things for her husband and family, but she doesn't realize that inside this big man is a person dying to be needed. I'm talking about wanting to be needed not by people at work but by his wife. What makes him feel needed? A clean house? No. A good meal? No. Those things

---

How My Life Changed

I grew up in a home where I was sexually abused by my stepfather. When I fell in love and got married after college, I tried to put the past behind me. But I still struggled. Every time Andrew touched me (he's a touchy sort of guy), I withdrew because images of my abuse would start running through my head.

After a year or so, Andrew just gave up. We lived in the same house, but as roommates, not lovers. It wasn't until a good friend took me with her to a seminar of yours that I understood what was going on. Andrew is a baby of the family whose language of love is touch. I'm a firstborn whose language of love is acts of service. When I finally understood that, I was able to go home and talk to Andrew. We cried together (yes, men can cry too) and agreed to go to counseling together.

It's been two months since then, and our marriage is completely different. Now we talk about things when they happen, and we're working on loving each other in the way we can receive it. Thanks for kicking off our marriage makeover.

Kendra, Wisconsin

---

make him feel served, but not *needed*. What makes most men feel needed and wanted is when their wives show them an active sexual interest.

Oh no, some of you women are thinking. *That again. Can't men think about anything other than sex?*

Sure we can! We think about food and ESPN too!

All kidding aside, the divorce statistics speak for themselves. Most men today do not feel needed. They are looking for significance, and fewer and fewer are finding that significance in the workplace. If a woman tunes in to the fact that her man needs to feel needed and that physical touch is a big part of that, she will increase the probability of becoming one with her mate . . . and keeping that mate for a lifetime.[2]

Men, you need to know that your wife wants what I call a "giving touch." That means an occasional loving touch that isn't tied to a sweaty and naked agenda. So often I hear women complain that what they really wanted to do was just hug their husband and give him a quick peck, but hubby got the wrong idea. The next thing the wife knows, her clothes are off and she's looking at the ceiling thinking, *This isn't exactly what I had in mind.*

So men, touch your wife gently, adoringly, and without asking for any touch in return. Take her hand occasionally when you go for a walk; slow down long enough to give her a quick peck on the cheek (or better yet, give her a tender kiss on the mouth). When she hugs you, hug her back. When she's sad or lonely or just tired, hold her, rub her feet, or just sit quietly next to her with your arm around her.

> *Touch has the power to do great harm or to communicate healthy affection. How are you using it in your relationships?*

If you're a parent, I need to share a few words with you too. Dr. Harry Schaumburg, who works with leaders on the problems of sexual misconduct and sexual addiction, warns, "Nearly all the sex addicts I've counseled have shared with me that their parents—or the people who raised them—were 'cold,' 'distant,' or 'didn't show much affection.' Through the years I've realized that appropriate physical touch plays a vital role in developing intimacy in relationships and in teaching appropriate physical boundaries, too. People tend to thrive physically and emotionally when they are nurtured with appropriate human touch. It helps to provide affirmation of love and acceptance as well as physical comfort."[3]

Touch has the power to do great harm or to communicate healthy affection. How are you using it in your relationships?

So . . . How Do I Figure It Out?

Some of you are thinking, *How can I figure out my spouse's or kid's love language when they won't talk to me, or when they don't even know it themselves?* It's simple. Ask yourself, *What does this person complain about most?*

Nine times out of ten, that complaint will revolve around the person's love language.

"Jerry's very good to me, Dr. Leman," one woman told me. "He brings me presents all the time, he fixes whatever gets broken, but he never wants to just sit with me. I can't tell you how much that hurts!"

I knew right away that that woman's love language was quality time, not receiving gifts or acts of service.

"Bob is happy to follow me around," another woman said, "but I wish he'd fix the broken lamp instead!" Right away, I knew she wanted to be loved with acts of service, not quality time.

> *Your goal is to learn how to love someone by expressing intimacy in a way that he or she can receive it.*

So open your ears to your loved ones, and they'll tell you how they want to be loved (even if they don't know it!). Make it your secret mission, and you'll be amazed what you find out.

Better yet, why not have a meaningful conversation at dinner tonight? If it's just you and your husband, or you and your boyfriend, or maybe your entire family (with kids), why not bring this book to the table, describe each love language, and ask each person to pick the one that means the most to them?

Keep in mind that your goal is to learn how to love someone by expressing affection in a way that he or she can receive it. Any of the love languages can be used to manipulate rather than love, but some are more open to abuse than others. I've seen some individuals supposedly love with acts of service—but they are actually covering up the fact that they have a difficult time being intimate with words or through touch. Giving gifts can have a built-in distance: "I'll give you flowers, but I won't talk to you. I won't give you myself." I'm not degrading these love languages. I just want you to be careful how you use them and that you're not using them to cover up a lack of love somewhere else.

Without understanding how others give and receive love, there's no way you can become the "new you" you long to be, because your relationships won't change. You will continue acting the same way toward a loved one—with the same results. And without understanding how *you* give and receive love, you won't be able to identify what you want and need to feel loved.

> *Imagine what a wonderful marriage you could have if you were both actively talking each other's love language!*

If You're Married . . .

No longer will you have to hope your husband or wife figures out your love language on their own. You'll be able to describe for them exactly what makes you feel loved. And if you have a smart spouse who wants "forever after" with you, they'll want to follow through to meet that need. Likewise, as you discover your loved one's need, you (being the smart person you are) will know how to fulfill it. Imagine what a wonderful marriage you could have if you were both actively talking each other's love language! I can guarantee that the atmosphere in your bedroom will go from humdrum boring to sizzling passion in a heartbeat.[4]

If You're Single or Single Again . . .

If you know how you like to be loved, you'll be better prepared to choose a suitable mate. For instance, if your love language is having someone spend quality time with you, don't marry a type A, Wall Street kind of guy. You'll just frustrate him and hurt yourself. If your love language is hearing words of affirmation, don't marry the silent, brooding type. (The fact that he brings you flowers every day won't mean a hill of beans to you in the future.)

It may sound cold and unromantic, but a fact's a fact. If you want a cuddly dog that will sit quietly on your lap, don't keep looking at Dobermans. If you want a dog that will protect you, stay away from the toy poodles. I don't subscribe to the theory that there's just one person made for each one of us and that "destiny" will bring us together. I think most of us could be happily married to any one of a number of people if we'd just focus on compatibility and common sense.[5]

> *If you want a dog that will protect you, stay away from the toy poodles.*

So how do you like to be loved? How do you tend to give love? As you identify your own love language—it might be a combination of languages or just one—you'll be well on your way to becoming a new you.

But the goal of this book isn't just to understand yourself; it's to understand yourself in the context of relationships. Your job is to get behind your loved ones' eyes and see what is important to them—what makes life worth living. And once you know that, why would you not want to make it happen for the ones you love?

When you begin to give love to others in the way they can accept it, it's amazing how relationships can change for the good—and a home can become a much friendlier place to hang out. You'll even gain the respect of neighbors and co-workers.

Why not try it and see?

What to Do on Thursday

1. Consider what you complain about. What's your love language?
2. Identify what those closest to you complain about. What are their love languages?
3. Brainstorm a few ways you could express your care to each person in his or her love language . . . then do one of them.

Friday

Shrink Thyself

You're the expert on yourself, so why not save $225 per session to see a professional shrink? (I'm sure you have better things to spend that money on.) I'll show you how.

This chapter is where you really get your money's worth. Instead of dropping thousands of dollars on expensive therapy, for the few bucks this book costs I'll take you through the new beliefs, attitudes, and actions that will help you reshape your personality for the better.

But there's one thing you have to do first.

You have to stop pretending. You won't have the energy to both create a false persona (that thin veneer you want people to see when they look at you) and improve your real persona (the person you know you are inside). Eventually, you're going to have to choose: *Do I really want to change, or do I want to keep pretending?*

> *All of us have two choices: build on who we are, or pretend to be someone else.*

All of us have two choices: build on who we are, or pretend to be someone else. Sadly, many of us spend a good bit of our day constructing a fake personality.

Are you? If so, let me ask you: why would you want to be someone else, anyway? You are unique—like a snowflake. You may not like the particular shape of your snowflake at times, but some of those oddities are what make you "you" . . . the only you in the universe.

So instead of spending all your time and energy trying to be something you're not, why not stop pretending?

By identifying your personality, by realizing your birth order and inherent strengths and weaknesses, by refusing to tell yourself lies (or to accept those creeping into your mind), and by knowing your love language, you've already become a new you. If you're not sure of that, just look back at where you were on Monday—and be amazed!

> *Give yourself a break. Lighten up!*

But the work isn't over. You've been the person you are for a long time. Now your job is to take what you've learned and move forward with a new determination not to dump on yourself. In other words, give yourself a break. Lighten up!

When I consider individuals who underwent real personal change, I always think of Steve Martin, one of my favorite actors.

A Wild and Crazy Guy

Actor Steve Martin was initially known best through his hit *Saturday Night Live* skit entitled "Two Wild and Crazy Guys." Along with Dan Aykroyd, Martin dressed in flashy outfits, talked obnoxiously, and basically made himself a very loud nuisance—with hilarious results. One of Martin's early comedy albums pictured him with balloons on his head on one side of the album, and an arrow running through his head on the other side. If it could get a laugh, Steve Martin would give it a try. He once skated across the stage of *The Tonight Show* wearing a King Tut outfit!

A clear Yorkie, if ever there was one.

Not surprisingly, Martin is the younger of two children. He had a knack for performance early on. As young as five years old, Martin was memorizing Red Skelton shows and performing them during show-and-tell at school. As a teenager, Martin worked at Disneyland and Knott's Berry Farm. He was the consummate class clown and was soon earning his living writing for well-known comedians, including the Smothers Brothers, Sonny and Cher, and Dick Van Dyke.

> *If it could get a laugh, Steve Martin would give it a try.*

In 1970 Martin decided to strike out on his own, performing stand-up comedy himself. His career took off six years later with *Saturday Night Live*, and a few years after that, his smash movie *The Jerk* established him as one of the most popular comedy performers of his day.

Of all Martin's movies, my personal favorite is the 1986 film *Three Amigos*. I've always thought that movie is worthy of five stars, and my family has watched it with me so many times I know almost the entire screenplay by heart. I can't tell you how thrilled I was to learn that *Three Amigos* may be one of Martin's favorite films as well. He told one magazine that *Three Amigos* is the rare film of his that he actually watched from start to finish and found himself "laughing his head off."[1]

It's interesting that throughout his life Martin has tried on wildly divergent personalities. If you were to slap the Yorkie label on him and leave it at that, you'd be sadly mistaken. Though he was a class clown, Martin earned straight As at Long Beach State College, planning to be a philosophy professor, of all things, but then dropped out of college to perform a stand-up routine of goofy gags and outrageous innuendo. He then went back to what one writer called his "straight arrow period." Martin cut his hair short, shaved off his facial hair, and appeared on stage in a white three-piece suit. That didn't last long. Martin soon went back to an outrageously funny style that could best be described as bizarre, and there he hit his stride.

> *Martin has always defied easy labeling.*

But following the megasuccess of *The Jerk*, Martin went serious again, starring in *Pennies from Heaven*, a very somber movie with a decidedly unhappy ending. While another string of comedies followed, Martin regularly retreated to more serious fare (such as *Grand Canyon* and *The Spanish Prisoner*). He wrote some critically praised plays, including *Picasso at the Lapin Agile*, as well as a novella entitled *Shopgirl*.

Those are the acts of a Great Dane or a Standard Poodle, not a lastborn Yorkie! While his outrageous acts fit the bill perfectly for a Yorkie, Martin has always defied easy labeling. He lives in a somewhat peculiar L-shaped building in Los Angeles with no front windows, a dwelling that Martin calls "the house that says 'Go away.'"[2]

This mixture of the outgoing Yorkie personality with the aloof, introverted streak is best seen in Martin's business cards. He doesn't like to sign autographs and mingle with fans, so instead he has signed business cards that read, "This certifies that you have had a personal encounter with me and that you found me warm, polite, intelligent and funny."[3]

It seems to me that Martin has Standard Poodle (perfectionistic) tendencies. He was once quoted as saying, "I [write] a little at a time. Sometimes it takes years to finish." He then displays his Yorkie nature in the same quote: "I never want to think it's work. If I thought I had to do some writing work, I'd just about die." Affirming his Yorkie quality again, Martin adds that comic acting comes naturally to him. "It's a wild gene," he says. "I guess I'm just a show-off."[4]

Steve Martin's words show how beneficial it is to become more aware of yourself. He recognizes that he wants to have fun. He doesn't want to think of writing as work, but he also realizes that he's about more than just having fun. He has a serious streak too. He's getting in touch with the blended aspects of his personality that we talked about in the Monday chapter.

Martin's example also shows us how a person can adapt his personality while still maintaining his true self. He calls his play *Picasso at the Lapin Agile* a "turning point in my life. . . . I remember seeing it a year later and thinking, 'I am really proud of this.'"[5] His success at writing plays has freed him up to pursue such diverse projects as writing an essay on playing the banjo for *The Oxford American* and an essay about a painter for *Art News*.

> **Lies You Tell Yourself**
>
> I can't change.
> I don't have time to change.
> I don't care what others think.
> I tried, but I just couldn't do it.

Part of this growth has to do with maturity. Martin explains, "I remember when I was younger, people would say something like, 'I don't care what they think.' I'd go: 'What do you mean by that? Because *I* care what they think.' And then you always hear older people say, 'I don't care what they think,' and you think, 'Yeah, you can do that when you get older.' And I started to understand that. You do start to not care what they think anymore. But you have to come to that. You have to go through a transition."[6]

Comics are passionately concerned about how others respond—their career depends on it. For Martin to confess that he cares less what others think is truly an impressive development. The class clown *can* cool off when it's appropriate to do so.

Are You Wine or Grape Juice?

One of the more profound influences on Martin's life was when his father and two close friends all died within a couple years of each other. During the same stretch, Martin also suffered a painful and somewhat messy divorce.

Maybe similar circumstances in your own life led you to pick up this book. A close friend died, you lost your job, a parent passed away, or a major life event occurred that shook you up and led you to begin thinking, perhaps for the very first time, about how you'll be remembered and what your priorities really are in life—and whether, like Scrooge on Christmas Eve, you have time to change.

> *Martin took three years off and decided to work on his personality.*

In response to the pressures in his life, Martin says, "[I] sort of changed myself, psychologically and professionally. I looked at what I was doing and I wasn't that fulfilled—in the movies. In the writing world I was very happy. In fact that kind of saved me emotionally, the fact I had *something* that I could be proud of."[7]

Martin took three years off and decided to work on his personality. Friends noticed a difference. "I think he got more open," director Frank Oz states. "He's become a warmer individual and more layered. I think he's become more wine than grape juice, which is a good thing."[8]

Isn't that a powerful statement? Wouldn't you like one of your friends to see such a maturing in you that they might say, "Yeah, Susan has become more wine than grape juice"?

Brian Grazer, a Hollywood producer, used to put up with Martin calling and saying, "Let's talk," but then hearing him say, 15 or 30 seconds later, "Okay, seeyalater!"[9]

That type of attitude is grape juice.

Now Martin has decided to hold a certain number of dinner parties every week with a rotating circle of friends, purposefully creating more of a social life for himself and going out of his way to invite non-Hollywood types to broaden his experience and his personality.

That type of attitude is wine.

Now in his midsixties, Martin has an opportunity to reevaluate how he has lived. "I wish I had paid as much attention to my personal life as I did to my professional life," he told one writer. "I didn't know how, but that's changing. The only regret I have is that I didn't learn things faster in life. I recently sat next to a woman who was in her 80s, and she said, 'Well, finally, you've become wise, and it's not too late.'"[10]

So Steve Martin is a work in progress. He has recognized some weaknesses in his life—superficiality in relationships, for example—and decided to make a change. Without losing his natural sense of humor—a true, priceless gift if ever there was one—Martin has deepened himself to also become known as "wise" by his friends.

> *"I wish I had paid as much attention to my personal life as I did to my professional life."*
> *—Steve Martin*

You, too, are a work in progress. What weaknesses in your life have you identified as a result of reading this book? What changes have you decided to make?

Breaking the Pattern

If you want to become a new you, you have to decide that you really want to change. You have to strip away your pretending persona and decide that you are going to be real—with yourself and with others. But none of that will matter if you don't catch this next important point.

I'd like to use a man named Wayne Carlson as an example. Wayne Carlson got off to a bad start. He was arrested and convicted for car theft when he was barely an adult—18 years old—and sentenced to one year at Saskatchewan's Prince Albert Penitentiary.

One year can seem like a long time to an 18-year-old, and jail is a rough place to live. For instance, cigarettes are forbidden (though they're smuggled in), so the only way you can light one is to wrap a fork with toilet paper and jam it into an exposed socket (hopefully without killing yourself in the process).

After several months, Carlson had had enough and decided to escape. He was successful but was later recaptured and sentenced to a longer period of time for escaping. The longer sentence only made Carlson more determined to get out of jail, so he escaped again. This went on for a North American record of 13 prison escapes. Carlson's initial one-year sentence eventually stretched into a three-decade ordeal.[11]

Wayne Carlson never wised up. His bad start turned into a bad habit that cost him three decades of living.

How about you? What bad starts and bad habits are keeping you from the life you want to live? The person you want to become?

The best definition of insanity I've ever read is "doing the same thing again and again while expecting different results." But isn't that what we do, over and over, when it comes to personality change? Like Wayne Carlson, we keep making the same mistakes, making a bad situation worse and often ruining our lives—and others' lives—in the process.

Do you know why people are willing to part with $225 to talk with a psychologist? They've made bad decisions. It's as simple as that. And the reason many are willing to keep paying $225 for months on end is that they keep making bad decisions and need an objective voice to help them break the pattern and hold them accountable.

I'll be blunt. Reading this book isn't going to do you one bit of good if you keep making the same kinds of poor decisions you've made in the past. You'll defeat yourself before you can even start changing for the better.

Like the woman in her late twenties who came to me for counseling because "life has been so unfair." The guy she'd moved in with had dumped her for another chick—after he'd created a baby. Fact is, she made a bad decision to hook up with the guy in the first place. (The old adage is true: you find who you're searching for.) And now she's going to have to live with the consequences. If she doesn't realize that it was her choices and actions that led to her present predicament, she'll continue hooking up with that same kind of guy. Before long, she'll have three or four kids, all with different fathers (none of whom can afford to make child-support payments, of course). By her fourth or fifth decade, her blonde cheerleader looks will have waned, she'll be left alone, and she'll continue thinking this world is terribly cruel and unfair.

But is it that the world is cruel and unfair—or that she made some awful choices that she now has to live with?

I can't tell you how many men have come to me, wanting me to fix their kids, when the men themselves are actually the ones who need fixing. After all, these men broke up their families for a younger woman or midlife freedom. And now they seem surprised—even angry—that their kids are displaying all the signs of insecurity, rebellion, and abandonment.

People who keep making the same mistakes usually have an ideal view of themselves that never squares with reality. So they base their choices on faulty assumptions—and continue to make poor choices. They continue to believe the lies they tell themselves about themselves.

> *The biggest lie you'll ever tell yourself is, "I'm going to try to do that." There's no trying. There's either doing it or not doing it.*

The biggest lie you'll ever tell yourself is, "I'm going to *try* to do that." There's no trying. There's either doing it or not doing it. Trying is a state of mind.

The difference between trying and doing? The level of commitment. It's easier to say, "I'm going to try to do that," because then there's a way out if you decide it's too hard and not worth all the work to follow through.

So if you're saying, "I'm going to try to do things differently in my life . . . uh, next month . . . uh, as part of my New Year's resolution . . . uh, next year, after I get a new job," you won't be going anywhere. But if you say, "Here are the things I'm going to change this week, here are the things I'm going to change next week, and here are the things I'm going to change next month," then you're going to do it!

Your Personal Makeover

If people like Steve Martin can launch a personality makeover, then why not you?

I've given you a lot of information to digest in this book. Hopefully you've hung with me through Monday, Tuesday, Wednesday, and Thursday. If not, and you just skipped to this end chapter, no fair! Go back and work your way through the chapters or you won't get the full benefit of the new you.

Today's the big day—the day you become the new you. The day you put everything together that we've talked about and decide that you will think and act in a new way that accomplishes the goal you set out to reach.

How will you accomplish this personal makeover?

Step #1: Look Back

You bought this book because you want to change something about yourself in the present that will change your future. For example, perhaps you want to find a diet that will stick and make you 30 pounds slimmer. Or you want to be the kind of person your husband wants to come home to, or the manager your co-workers will respect. But the only way you can positively impact your future is to become more aware of your past, so that you can make different—and better—choices.

So the first step to any change? Looking back.

That's what I did my senior year in high school. All my class-mates were talking about going to college and university. While they were excited about their plans, I was sad. It dawned on me that this wonderful little family of people in our small town wouldn't spend the rest of their lives hanging out at Jack's hot-dog stand on Friday nights. "You mean I won't see Jim the dork walk around with ketchup on the corner of his mouth all night, oblivious to the fact that everyone sees what he doesn't?" I asked myself one day. "You mean Jill won't always stand outside Gordy's car, wearing her pink cashmere sweater and flipping that beautiful mane of golden hair? You mean Moonhead and I won't keep giving John wedgies and making everyone laugh by running little Dickie's underwear up the school flagpole? All that is gonna stop?"

Suddenly the thought occurred to me: *I've been a fool. I've spent four years in high school entertaining my classmates, largely because of my own insecurities. But what have all those antics gotten me? Nothing. My friends are getting ready to build a fu-ture, and me? Well, I'm looking at nothing . . . except the frightening reality of classic underachievement.*

I can't tell you how important it was for me to look back at where my past actions had gotten me—and why. If all I had done was look ahead—thinking who I could en-tertain the next year—I would have been like Charlie Brown, who really did believe that this time it would be different. This time Lucy wouldn't pull the football away from him just before he kicked it. Based on the past, Charlie had no reason to believe anything Lucy told him, but he never looked back. He only looked forward and fell on his backside every single time.

> *Charlie had no reason to believe anything Lucy told him, but he never looked back. He only looked forward and fell on his backside every single time.*

Once I took an honest (and painful) look back, I was willing to admit I had to do some things differently. Thank God for that schoolteacher, Miss Wilson. She showed me that maybe I could use those off-the-wall, comical antics to do good someday.

She was right. I believe that one of the reasons I frequently have standing-room-only attendance in my seminars is that I'm driven to make sure everyone is having fun. That does wonders for word-of-mouth publicity.

This philosophy covers just about everything I do. For instance, I once appeared on a nationally syndicated radio show that most authors drool over, though few get invited to. The reason so many writers want to be on this show is that just one appearance can make your book sales take off. Appearing two days in a row is a dream. But the producers booked me for three full programs. Why? Well, I must have had something to say, but I think it also comes back to the fact that they have a good time when I'm on the air. Whenever I appear on *The View* or the *Today* show, my gauge of success isn't, "What did the host think?" but rather, "Did I get the camera crew to laugh?" If the production people are holding their sides, I'm thinking, *This is working!* and I know I'm going to be invited back.

> **5 Ways to Guarantee Success . . . at Anything**
> 1. Set a goal.
> 2. Keep your goal reasonable. (Don't bite off more than you can chew.)
> 3. Don't second-guess yourself.
> 4. Don't listen to the naysayers.
> 5. As Winston Churchill said during a time of war, "Never give up."

The key is to look back and understand the basic strengths you bring to life, and then figure out how to put them to better use and use them for different purposes. I'm still the class clown, but now I've learned to use that skill to succeed in life rather than to get myself in trouble.

Steve Martin was always a person of depth, but he realized as a lastborn Yorkie that he was also naturally funny and able to write comedy. Even a comedic writer is still a writer, and Martin chose to build on that to create a career as a novelist and essayist as well as an actor.

In short, Martin has not allowed himself to be boxed in. He has looked back, built on his strengths, and then continued to stretch himself and develop his personality, capitalizing on his history to create an even more promising future. You can do the same.

Step #2: Take Baby Steps

Next to *Three Amigos,* my favorite five-star movie is *What about Bob?* In this classic comedy, Leo Marvin (played by Richard Dreyfuss) has just written a smash bestseller entitled *Baby Steps,* when he runs into the neurotic of all neurotics, Bob (played by Bill Murray).

> *I'm still the class clown, but now I've learned to use that skill to succeed in life rather than to get myself in trouble.*

One of the humorous things about this movie is how they make fun of a book title that actually makes very good sense: mental health and personal change are both best pursued through baby steps. Some people become intent on making a change but then go about it in the wrong way. Instead of working steadily toward progress, they seek to make colossal jumps, which virtually guarantees failure. Then they say, "See, I knew I would fail. I shouldn't even try."

How are you going to do things differently?

Begin making many different choices on a day-to-day basis. There is no silver bullet. You need an entire arsenal consistently at your disposal. As St. Paul says, "I tell myself not to do these things, but I still do these things" (the Leman translation). The crux behind any behavioral change is first looking back and admitting that what you've been doing in the past hasn't

> *How are you going to do things differently?*

worked—that's what we covered in step #1—and then making many small changes to go someplace different.

For example, let's take June, a classic pleaser who came to see me out of exhaustion. This woman says yes even when she means no. She lets other people virtually run her life, and whenever anything goes wrong she immediately accepts the blame, even if it wasn't her fault. She can't bear to disappoint anyone, which makes her miserable, as she leaves no time for herself and consents to a schedule that runs her ragged.

For June, there is no magic bullet. What does June need to do to become the person she really wants to be? She needs to stop saying yes when she means no—beginning today. And she needs to learn how to say no. Since pleasers are worried first and foremost about offending others, their "no" is usually pretty wishy-washy. So she needs to find a different way to communicate.

Here's what I told her: "After you've been asked to do something that you know you shouldn't do, I want you to start your statement with the word *no*. Got that? The first word out of your mouth has to be 'No,' as in 'No, I'm unable to help you.' When Patricia from the PTA starts talking about how good you are at running the carnival, you don't say, 'Well, Patricia, I'd really like to help, but . . .' Instead, you say, 'No, Patricia, I'm unable to help this year.' And whatever you do, don't give any excuses."

June started to squirm in her chair. "But why, Dr. Leman?"

"Because when you give an excuse—'I'd like to help, but Jack is working overtime, and our daughter has started dance and has lots of recitals, and I just don't have the time to run the entire carnival'—you give Patricia time to say, 'What if I got Lisa to help you out this year? She's so good at decorating and managing her time.' Patricia can yank on your pleaser's strings like a master marionette operator, and before long you'll feel like a helpless puppet who has just agreed to do one more thing you don't have time to do. So cut all that out. Simply say, 'No, I'm unable to help this year.'"

Now before June can claim victory, she's going to have to repeat this process many times. She doesn't stop being a pleaser with one visit to my office. She has to learn, through a series of baby steps, how to say no. If she's really neck-deep in being a pleaser, she may even have to begin by picking and choosing who she stands up to. For instance, instead of her mother-in-law, she might practice saying no to a telemarketer on the phone. The important thing for her to recognize is that change is a long process.

A friend of mine has suffered with depression most of his adult life. I was near his hometown while on a business trip and decided to stop by to see him. My visit was personal. I was just being his friend, not his shrink. As soon as he opened the door, though, I knew he needed help. He must have had three or four days' growth of beard on his face.

"Jim, are you growing a beard?" I asked later, after we had caught up a bit.

"No," Jim responded in a very slow, depressed tone.

"Can I give you a simple suggestion, just as a friend?"

"Sure."

How My Life Changed

I've lived a rough life—much of it my own fault. Then, six months ago, I heard you talk on the radio about perfectionism. People who know me would never guess it (my apartment's a mess), but you described me perfectly. I had no idea I was a frustrated perfectionist, but when I thought about everything you'd said, it all made sense. I'm a firstborn, and I could never be perfect enough for my parents. So, as soon as I turned 18, I lit out from home and never went back. Let's just say I didn't do myself any favors in my lifestyle.

But then I heard you, and I realized for the first time that I was spending my life trying to get back at my parents (I haven't spoken to them in nine years). I'm now taking baby steps back toward the kind of life I want to live . . . the person I want to be. I'm not sure I'll ever have the courage to talk to my parents again, but one thing I know: for the first time in my life, I like me.

Jake, Washington DC

"Tomorrow morning when you get up, shave."

It may sound stupid and trite for me to offer such basic advice for depression, but all this goes back to baby steps. Even when you're depressed and you don't feel like shaving or washing your hair or taking a shower, sometimes you still need to force yourself to do those mundane things. Over time those seemingly mundane tasks become profound steps toward long-term personality change.

This same principle holds true whether you're trying to curb destructive eating habits, inappropriate sexual behavior, or any personality trait you want changed. If you know you talk too much at dinner, decide that the next time you eat with a group of people, you'll cut down your talking by 25 percent. Force yourself to be quiet, to listen, and to pay attention to others.

Practice may not make us perfect, but if you believe in the magic bullet, you might as well believe in the tooth fairy. Both will get you the same thing—nothing!

Step #3: Improve Your Self-Talk

In that five-star movie *Three Amigos*, there's a hilarious scene in which Steve Martin's character finds himself in a terrible predicament with chains on both his wrists and his ankles. He goads himself forward to try to get free and repeats, "Gonna make it, gonna make it, gonna make it." But just before he gets to the point where he could grab the lever that would free him, he gets slammed back against the wall.

Life can be like that sometimes, can't it? You think you're just about there—you've lost eight pounds and are really eating better—when you're invited to your niece's wedding. That day, you eat particularly light—one small bowl of oatmeal for breakfast and a salad for lunch. Since you've been doing so well, you give yourself permission to have one little piece of cake. Fifteen minutes later, you've had three pieces, so you say, "I've already blown it, so what the heck? I might as well have a fourth piece."

206

Setbacks are going to come. It's not a matter of *if*, it's a matter of *when*. Have you developed the skills to talk yourself through times of failure?

For example, a woman trapped in a cycle of failure would say to herself, *I've blown it. Three pieces! How could I be so stupid? I'll always be fat. Well, if I'm going to be fat, one more piece of cake won't make any difference. In fact, another piece of cake might make me feel better.*

> Setbacks are going to come. It's not a matter of if; it's a matter of when.

A woman who learns the skills I'm talking about would think instead, *Okay, I probably shouldn't have had that second piece, and yes, a third piece sounds even better. But I've been doing very well, and I've worked very hard. Two pieces won't kill me. I don't want to eat a third, however, because that's the type of thing I did when I was losing control. I need to walk away from this table and find someone to talk to. Oh, there's Martha. She's always an encouraging person. I think I'll go over to her, away from this table.*

This isn't just theory to me. I've had to live it out in my own life.

One of my favorite pastimes is eating pumpkin pie. One night while we were out for dinner, Sande all of a sudden got that startled look like she'd just remembered something. It turns out we had company coming for dinner the next night. She had to get up early and decorate for an event at church, and that meant she didn't have time to make dessert from scratch, which is her specialty. So she told me, "Leemie, you have to do me a big favor. Tomorrow morning you have to go to Marie Callender's and pick up two pies—one pumpkin pie and one lemon meringue pie."

The next morning, when I arrived at the store, I discovered that they had a special on pumpkin pies, so I decided to buy two pumpkin pies and one lemon meringue. When I got home, the house was empty. It was 11:00 a.m. and I hadn't had time for breakfast that morning. Well, I looked down at the table and realized I had an extra pumpkin pie just sitting there. A piece of that pie with a little whipped cream would taste great with a cup of coffee.

I cut a generous slice and held it in my hand instead of using a fork. That was my first mistake. I ate it by chomping on it, not by tasting it. Boy, that first piece went down too easily, too quickly. Somehow my brain hadn't registered that I'd already eaten one rather generous piece of pumpkin pie. Besides that, my taste buds were going wild. That pie wasn't just good—it was near perfection.

> *My taste buds were going wild. That pie wasn't just good—it was near perfection.*

I was thinking, *You know, that sucker was so good, and it brings the best out of my cup of coffee. I might just do an encore.*

Time for act two. I cut another piece, this one slightly larger. After all, no use selling myself short! The second piece went down just as easily as the first. I looked at the pie, three-eighths of which was gone, but I still had more coffee to drink and nothing to go with it.

I'll take just a one-inch slice to help me finish off my coffee, I thought, but a one-inch slice of pie is like finger food. One direct hit to the tongue and it was gone. I did that several times until two-thirds of the pie had disappeared.

Now I had a heck of a dilemma. My brain was finally catching up to my stomach, screaming out, *Overload! Overload!*

But I also had another bigger problem. Sande would be home shortly, and she'd see that there was no one in the house but me. And what would I tell her? "Uh, honey, the pie thief stopped at our house and ate over half the pie, then I just helped with the rest"?

Uh-oh, my conscientious self said. *I overdid it.*

You know, Leman, there's a way around this, my alter ego said.

What's that?

Eat the evidence.

I found the logic compelling. With one simple slice of the knife, I divided what was left of the pie into two pieces and wolfed both of them down. To my credit, I didn't put any whipped cream on the last pieces.

In short, I ate the whole pie. I could hardly move, but I knew I was committed now and had to destroy all evidence, including the foil pie tin, so I stashed that in the bottom of the trash.

I sat down for a while, paying dearly and uncomfortably for my choices, until Sande walked through the front door about 20 minutes later.

"Hi, honey," she said. "Did you get the pies?"

"Yeah, they're on the counter."

"I'm going to make a fresh pot of coffee. Would you like a cup?"

"Sure."

Then Sande yelled from the kitchen, "This pie smells so good and would taste delicious with your cup of coffee. Would you like me to cut you a slice?"

"Oh, no, honey," I said, my stomach bursting against its skin, "I gotta really start watching what I eat."

You see, I'm just as weak as you are, only I may have bigger and worse failures. I've had to learn to make the little choices, just like you do.

The next time, instead of just letting things happen, pause for a moment, think through what is taking place, and then self-talk your way out of it. When people face personality ruts and addictions, most often they're simply reacting—they hit upon *Don't just do something— stand there!* a stimulus (delicious wedding cake or fabulous pumpkin pie) and let the collapse happen without using their brain as the powerful tool it can be.

I like to use phrases that shock people into seeing truth in a new way. One of those phrases is, "Don't just do something—stand

209

there!" The cliché, of course, is just the opposite: "Don't just stand there—do something!" But if you're facing a personality rut, you need to pull back from the action and carefully talk your way through your next several steps.

Another good strategy behind positive self-talk is continually reminding yourself that even if you're not losing weight, you have other good things going on: your family, your work, your friendships, etc. So what will you choose to focus on? The one thing you're failing at? Or the seven things that are going right? There will always be one thing in life that isn't going perfectly, but mentally healthy people learn to keep perspective by thinking about those things that lift them up and give them hope.

Step #4: Marshal Your Imaginative Energy

Eileen came to see me because she'd tried numerous times to lose weight and had failed.

"You really want to lose weight?" I asked her.

"Of course I do," she said. "That's why I'm here."

I handed her a blank three-by-five card. "There you go," I said. "That's your key."

She looked at me like I had an arrow through my head. "What am I supposed to do with this?"

"I want you to write your current weight on it, date it, and then post it on your refrigerator door. It'll read like this: 'On January 25, 2010, my weight is 205.'"

"But everyone can see it there!"

"Exactly!" I said. "That's the point."

Now Eileen really thought I was crazy.

"And while you're at it," I said, "why don't you take a second card? You can post this one on your desk at work."

Not everyone takes me up on this suggestion, but those who do find it to be tremendously beneficial. They're worried about being embarrassed, but can I be honest with you? If you weigh over 200 pounds, everyone already knows it. Your weight is no secret, and frankly, whether they put you at 225 or 215, do you think it really matters to them? Probably not. But it matters to you, and when you publicly post your weight, you're beginning to marshal the power of your imaginative energy.

Most people spend half the day denying their problems. When they put their problem right in front of them, denial is shattered and they're finally able to do something about it.

> *Most people spend half the day denying their problems.*

I do this myself. When I went to the doctor, he took my vitals and sighed.

"What is it, Doc?" I asked.

"Dr. Leman, your blood pressure is getting dangerously high. I'm afraid you're going to have to start watching what you eat."

Being in my sixties, with a daughter who has yet to graduate from high school, I'd kinda like to hang around a little longer, if for no other reason than to give the man who wants to marry Lauren a really hard time when he comes to ask me for her hand. Since Lauren has three older sisters (Krissy and her boyfriend, Dennis, got to be the guinea pigs when he asked for her hand), I figure I'll have lots of practice by then and can really give the guy a memory or two. For this and other reasons, I have ample motivation to truly care about the state of my blood pressure.

The problem is, blood pressure doesn't have an immediate effect on my life; it's the type of thing I know I should address someday. And when I leave my office in the middle of the afternoon, feel my stomach start churning, and pass an Arby's with a big sign advertising its bacon double-cheese cordon-bleu sandwich . . . well, *that's* immediate pressure. It's like my car is steering itself right into the drive-through.

So I took one of my doctor's cards, flipped it over, and wrote my blood pressure on it. I then taped it to my dashboard. Every morning that number is one of the first things I see. At lunchtime I see those numbers again. After work, on my way home, they're staring me in the face, helping me to drive past Arby's, go home, and get a bowl of cereal with skim milk instead of the bacon double-cheese cordon-bleu sandwich that looks, I must admit, far more appealing. But the cereal can hold me until dinner.

The thing I like about this exercise is that it not only marshals my imaginative energy, it also marshals the energy of my family and friends. When an associate drives with me to lunch, he'll invariably comment on that card: "What the heck is that?"

"My blood pressure."

"Sheesh, Cubby, you better lay off the peanut butter!"

"I know. That's why I put the card there."

So when we get into the restaurant and I start to look at the wrong part of the menu, my associate, my wife, or one of my kids will often smile, repeat the number on that card, and point me toward the salads and low-fat alternatives.

Cards like mine are just simple tools that remind you of where you want to go. They show you're serious about changing.

If you have children and your kids have decided they want to remain virgins until their wedding night (and I hope they have), they can post a card on their dresser mirror or car dashboard: "I'm worth waiting for." If a guy ever gets in your daughter's bedroom or car, he'll immediately know your child's goals—waiting until marriage.

Most of the families who ask me questions during seminars or radio programs have no port of call. That is, they don't have a safe harbor to run to or a strategy for beating back life's inevitable pressures and temptations. Consequently, when the waves hit, many capsize. While I've never run a marathon myself (if I ever want to feel that kind of pain, I'll simply ask one of my kids to hit me repeatedly with a two-by-four and save myself the blisters), I've talked to people who have, and the successful ones all say the same thing: "You better begin the race with some strategies if you want to complete it." You have to think about the moments of decision ahead of time—what you'll do if you feel tired at 10 miles, how you'll respond if you feel you're slipping behind your pace and feeling unusually tired at 18 miles, etc.

A young man who won his state's high school championship race in the mile impressed his coach with the way he marshaled his imaginative energy. "If I get boxed out in the first lap, this is what I'm going to do," he told his coach on the way to the meet. "I'll work my way to the outside, but make sure I look over my shoulder so I don't trip. If the pace is slow, I'm going to take the lead. If it's too fast, I'm going to hold back but still maintain contact. By the third lap, I want to be right on Rob Waller's heels. . . ." He used his imaginative energy to think about every potential problem so that when it arose he'd know exactly what to do.

If you want to change yourself, you need to use this same power. Marshal your imaginative energy.

Let's go back to Eileen, the woman who wanted to lose weight. In addition to her publicly posting those numbers, I helped her develop some strategies.

"You know yourself, Eileen. You know your downfall. What is it that really puts on the weight? What's your favorite treat at night?"

"That's easy. Breyer's mint chocolate chip ice cream with chocolate sauce."

"Who brings the ice cream home?"

"I do."

"So what do you think is a good strategy?"

"Not buying the ice cream in the first place."

"That's an improvement, but what will you do when the ice cream craving hits?" (See, I know this stuff, because I've lived it too.)

Eileen smiled. "Probably go out and buy some."

"Of course you will. Tell me, do you like sherbet?"

"Yeah, but not as much as ice cream."

"Me neither. But why don't you buy a pint container of sherbet the next time you're at the grocery store? Instead of going completely cold turkey, when you get the ice cream craving you can give yourself a small single scoop of sherbet. And let's see if we can't make that pint of sherbet last at least seven to ten days, okay?"

Let me tell you—if Eileen can substitute a half gallon of ice cream with a pint of sherbet, she will have made great progress. But to get there, she'll have to devise a strategy ahead of time. She'll have to marshal her imaginative energy.

Step #5: Know Your Destination

In addition to knowing your problem (overtalkativeness, impatience, gossip, etc.), you need to know your solution. When my doctor told me what was wrong with my blood pressure numbers, he gave me better numbers to shoot for. If I want to lose a few pounds, I want to know not only where I am now but also where I hope to be in two or three months. Without a goal, there's no way I'm going to get anywhere.

The best way to treat a vice is to plant an opposing virtue. Here's what I mean.

One of my daughters once found herself caught up in an ugly middle school game—gossip. Gossip can be a disease among teenage girls, and it can spread like liquid butter on a piece of hot toast. My daughter found herself joining in, but one night she confessed how guilty it made her feel.

"Daddy, I know it's wrong to talk bad about someone behind their back, but sometimes it seems like I can't help myself. I want to join in the talk and be a part of the group. What else can I do?"

My daughter wasn't dumb. She knew that if everyone always gossiped about everyone else, it was only a matter of time until she herself got slammed—if she hadn't already. Plus she felt miserable the next time she saw one of the girls she'd gossiped about.

I listened, then said, "Honey, why don't you be different?" Unfortunately, *different* is not a word that middle school girls cherish, so I added, "Would you be willing to try a little experiment?

I don't want you to feel guilty, and I think this will help you make even more friends."

"Okay, Daddy."

"Try planting a virtue wherever there's a vice."

Her brow crinkled. "Uh, what?"

"What's the opposite of gossip?"

"I'm not sure."

"Well, if you heard someone talking about you, would you want to hear negative things or positive things?"

"Positive, I guess."

"Sure you would. So here's what I want you to do. Why don't you talk to Megan about Shawna, but get Megan to say something positive. Bait her: 'Megan, don't you think Shawna has pretty hair?' That type of thing. Megan will agree with you if you keep giving her opportunities. Then your job is to go to Shawna and say, 'I heard Megan talking about you this morning.' 'Oh yeah?' Shawna will ask. 'What did she say?' At first Shawna will be suspicious, thinking it's something negative, but you'll get to surprise her by saying, 'She was telling me how sweet you are and how much she loves that outfit you wore yesterday.' Then Shawna will probably compliment Megan right back."

> *The best way to treat a vice is to plant an opposing virtue.*

"How do you know?"

"I'm a psychologist, honey, trust me. She'll say something like, 'Shawna is so encouraging. And I just love that new haircut she got last week,' and you know what you'll do next, right?"

"I'll tell Megan what Shawna said?"

"That's right! Do that with the worst gossips. Help them feel how wonderful it is to discover encouragement instead of gossip."

My daughter went to her classmates and put this experiment to work. It was an unqualified success. While there were still occasional gab sessions, overall the friends took a big step toward encouragement rather than character assassination.

You can do the same thing. Instead of simply telling yourself, *I don't want to yell at the kids*, figure out a positive response: *I'm going to set firm guidelines. If the guidelines aren't followed, I won't yell. Instead, I'll calmly inform them of the consequences, which they were told about ahead of time. There will be no discussion and no argument—just clear guidelines and clear consequences.*[12]

Craig came to me because he was struggling with pornography. My goal? To get him to put the same amount of energy, time, and money into his romantic relationship with his wife that he used to spend on porn. "Why don't you take all the money you'll save from not calling 1-900 numbers and bring home some completely unexpected flowers for your wife? Instead of spending an evening in a strip club, why don't you arrange to have a babysitter and take your wife to a nice hotel?"

Men who carry on "extracurricular" activities have to plan how to cover their tracks, and the sex industry isn't cheap. Men can drop hundreds of dollars a month on this addiction. They complain that their wife isn't interested, but if they would spend the same amount of time planning a romantic evening for her as they do planning an excuse to get away surreptitiously, they might find that the climate at home would change.

If you're too harsh with your kids, focus on becoming gentler. If you talk too much in a group, focus on becoming a good listener. If you are too shy, plan to introduce yourself to at least three people you've never met at the next party you attend.

In short, know where you want to go, and take small steps to get there.

Step #6: Give Yourself Room to Fail

Ichiro Suzuki made headlines around the world in 2001 when he became the first position player from Japan to win a full-time spot with a major league baseball team (the Seattle Mariners). The headlines kept coming when Ichiro hit an astonishing .360 his first two months of the season, at that point having the second-highest batting average of anyone in the American league!

But think about this: what does a .360 batting average mean? It means that Ichiro gets a hit roughly one out of three times—a little more than that, but not much. Almost no one gets a hit four out of ten times over the course of a season, which means baseball greatly reveres people who fail at the plate roughly two-thirds of the time.

The all-or-none theory—"I'll quit once for all"—rarely works. When someone lives by this philosophy, what often happens is that they quit smoking successfully for a couple weeks, then the roof falls in—financial pressure, a smart-mouthed kid, a tough time at work—and in near desperation, they light up

> *The all-or-none theory—"I'll quit once for all"— rarely works.*

a cigarette. The person who lives by the all-or-none theory thinks, *Well, I blew it. I had a cigarette, I ruined the whole thing, so I might as well go back to smoking.*

I'm suggesting you have an entirely different response. Encourage yourself with these words: "I went two weeks without a cigarette! I wish I could have gone two months, but two weeks is a good start. Though I messed up today, tomorrow's a new day, and I'll do better then."

A baseball player doesn't quit trying after one strikeout or even a series of strikeouts. In fact, it's not uncommon for players having a great year to go through occasional slumps. In the first year of his famous $25-million-a-year contract, Texas Ranger Alex Rodriguez Jr. was having a sensational season. He led the American League in home runs, was right up there for runs batted in, and had a very respectable .333 batting average. But during one series with his former team, A. Rod batted 1–10, or .100. That means he created an out nine times out of ten! But no one thought he should quit. No one said, "He's lost it." Baseball teaches us to handle failure and move on. So does life.

> *One flub doesn't mean the entire program is wrecked. It just means you're human. You need to collect your strength and give it one more go.*

Remember baby steps? That's what you need. Ever see babies walk? They go backwards sometimes. You will too. One flub doesn't mean the entire program is wrecked. It just means you're human. You need to collect your strength and give it one more go.

Step Up to the Vision!

Apparently Steve Martin picked up a lot of this stuff on his own. His biographer, Morris Walker, writes:

Just as Steve has blasted into the galaxy of stars, he is imploding into the microcosm. The bigger he gets, he still manages to "get small." It's interesting to note that since Steve made it big, his personal letterhead had a simple Helvetica type face at the top of the page, which read "Steve Martin" in clear, embossed, capital letters. Then, around 1990, Steve's traditional letterhead changed. He still had that same simple "STEVE MARTIN" at the top of his beige linen stationery that he used for 25 years, but this new letter I received had a new phrase:

STEVE MARTIN
"Finally, someone with a vision"

. . . Anyone who ever worked with Steve, saw him perform, or watched him attempt to do anything he set his mind to was keenly aware of Steve's vision. It's tunnel vision. But as I've mentioned many times in these pages, Steve is a very private person. His tunnel vision is an obvious manifestation of his aspirations. It's the method by which he accomplishes anything and everything. . . . The distant light at the end is only a glimmer to even the greatest visionary. Only Steve sees his visions as they will one day exist.[13]

Do you have that same vision? Are you willing to build on what you are, toward what you aren't yet—but you want to be?

And are you willing to put a little muscle into it?

While Fred Astaire was certainly graceful, wonderfully charming, and perhaps one of the best dancers ever to come out of Hollywood, the truth is, he wasn't born that way. He worked at it, and he worked hard.

One day before an Academy Awards ceremony in which he was scheduled to receive a lifetime achievement Oscar, Astaire spent the better part of an afternoon practicing getting out of his seat and bounding up the stairs onto the stage to receive his award. The night of the awards ceremony, millions of viewers saw a very gifted dancer seemingly glide effortlessly up those steps; what they never saw was the practice that went into the creation of such a "natural" effort.[14]

> *We all want to change. But not all of us have the courage or the vision to do so.*

The new you can be practiced in the same way. At first, patience may not come naturally to you. You might be more inclined to gossip than to encourage. You might have a difficult time holding back from talking about yourself, or you might be too shy or too aggressive. But if you practice like Astaire did, if you put the principles we've already talked about into play, eventually you can create the best version of yourself. As flawed and imperfect as you are, you can move forward in life as you step up to the vision of the person you want to become.

And here's the most amazing thing of all: if there's a sense of realness about you, others will seek you out. They may even ask your counsel as they see you changing. You see, underneath everything, all of us are dissatisfied with some aspect of ourselves in some way. We all want to change. But not all of us have the courage or the vision to do so.

But you? Your time is now!

You know your personality—your strengths and your weaknesses. You know the traits of your birth order. You've explored your early childhood memories as well as those sneaky lies you tell yourself, and you've decided you're no longer going to fall for them. You know what your love language is and why knowing yours and others' love languages is so important. And you have vision. You understand who you are and where you've been, and you know where you're going. You've become an expert on yourself through the six steps—and you're guaranteed to gain the new you for a lifetime.

You are indeed ready to achieve your full potential. The new you is not only in the future; the new you is here, now!

And I'm smiling all over at seeing how far you've come.

What to Do on Friday

1. Decide that this time you *will* change. There's no more trying. There's only doing.
2. Pinpoint your destination. (How can you get there if you don't know what it is?)
3. Strip away any facade. Decide to be real.
4. Stop dumping on yourself.
5. Look back so you can move forward.
6. Give yourself room to fail.

Bonus Section for the Curious

How the New You Works

In relationships, at work . . . your life can be transformed with
these quick suggestions.

Getting a Handle on the New You

You now know what your personality is, or what blend of personalities you are.

And that has helped you get a handle on *who* you are.

You also know what birth order you are—numerically, which
of course was easy to figure out, but also functionally, which most
likely took additional investigation on your part. And that has
helped you get a clearer picture of *why* you are the way you are.

You've also figured out how you responded to your personality and birth order, as well as the events you experienced in your
childhood, to form your own private logic—your view of yourself
and the world.

And you pinpointed your love language—the way you best like to give and receive love.

Now how can you specifically use what you've learned?

The New You in Relationships

Whether you're single or married, understanding personality, birth order, your early childhood memories, and the love languages can play a valuable role in teaching you both how to love and how to find the right person to love. This information can help you be a better parent too.

If You're Single or Single Again . . .

If you're single or single again, you're standing at a pivotal place. It's like standing at a train crossing, looking to the left and then to the right for oncoming trains, as well as watching for flashing lights that warn of impending danger. If you choose to ignore that protective gate that comes down before the train reaches the station, and you step across those tracks, you're likely to get run over.

Now's the time to stop, look, and listen.

So now's the time to stop, look, and listen.

Look back on your life and your dating patterns for a minute. Then ask yourself this question: *When it comes to relationships, how have I done?* If your relational life is a mess, I'm willing to bet that you have based most of your previous decisions on feelings. You were convinced that this man or this woman was "the one," your destined soul mate. The tingling way you felt when you first kissed convinced you that "this is the person I'm going to spend the rest of my life with."

So how did that work out for you? Probably not well. If you picked up this book, you picked it up for a reason—because you want to make a change.

Are you willing to do something different? To some of you, what I'm going to say next will sound terribly unromantic. But just hear me out. I think I can help you make a much better choice when you consider another— or your first—life partner.

For instance, let's say you're a lastborn. By now you know your weaknesses—jumping into the water with both feet and then discovering it's boiling around you. As a baby of the family, you likely have a difficult time reining in your compulsive tendencies. You

> *My rule of thumb concerning birth order is this: marry your opposite.*

probably like to be on center stage or at least well cared for. You may have a special gift for spending money—even, on occasion, money you don't have. Did I peg you right?

Tell me, what will happen if you marry someone just like you— that is, another lastborn? Nine times out of ten, disaster! You'll be broke; the house will erupt into chaos; the bills will go unpaid; and your happy-go-lucky nature will take a severe downslide into discouragement, perhaps even depression.

As a lastborn myself, I can tell you that one of the best decisions I've ever made was to marry my firstborn wife. My rule of thumb concerning birth order is this: marry your opposite. Two firstborns create more sparks than the Fourth of July. Two lastborns may have a lot of fun initially but eventually lose their way. Two middleborns may never be able to make a decision without worrying about offending the other person.

> *Middle children are like Type O blood—they go along with just about anything, except perhaps another middle.*

This means that the ideal marriage arrangements are lastborn-firstborn or lastborn-only. So what about the middles? Middle children are like Type O blood—they go along with just about anything, except perhaps another middle. Keep in mind that there are different types of middles. A middleborn man who also happens to be the oldest son might be a very good choice for a lastborn wife—but the same guy may butt heads with a firstborn wife. A middleborn woman who is the youngest girl in her family could be an ideal match for a firstborn male—but maybe not the best choice for a lastborn male.

Look at the entire family situation and learn to make a wise choice. Marry your opposite, and you can't go too far wrong.

> **Lies You Tell Yourself**
>
> We're in love—it'll all work out!
>
> Once we're married, he'll change.
>
> Every day will be as romantic as this one.

The same principle holds true for Great Danes, Standard Poodles, Irish Setters, and Yorkies. In general, you'll do better by marrying your opposite. Some Irish Setters get along better with a Yorkie—their quiet, peaceful nature relies on someone else who has spunk—while others may prefer a Great Dane or Standard Poodle who will take charge.

You'll see sparks fly or gaps arise if two Great Danes get into a relationship—or two Yorkies, two Standard Poodles, or two Irish Setters. I've already stated that I see most lastborns as Yorkies, most middleborns as Irish Setters, most Standard Poodles as only children, and most Great Danes as firstborns. This isn't 100 percent accurate, of course, so learn to look at yourself in balance—for instance, a lastborn with Yorkie tendencies but also a bent toward being a Great Dane. If that's the case, consider marrying an Irish Setter. If you're a lastborn with Irish Setter tendencies, look for a Standard Poodle or Great Dane.

Before you romantics start howling at how unromantic this sounds, let me just say this: I have counseled—formally and informally—thousands of couples, almost all of whom were head over heels in love with each other, giddy at the thought of spending the rest of their lives together. The romance was there; the sexual chemistry was high; they couldn't keep their hands off each other.

But they made a bad match. Once the infatuation wore off—and it always will—they were left with an ill-considered choice and a difficult marriage.

How My Life Changed

You just saved me from making a huge mistake. I'd spent a year dating this guy and was sure I was in love with him. I was waiting for the day he'd ask me to marry him. Then I heard you talk on *Good Morning America* about relationships and got hit over the head. When I asked myself your relationship questions, I realized Chris was not the kind of guy I'd want to spend the rest of my life with. Sure, he was a prize catch (at least the girls at my health club thought so), but he wasn't for me.

Thanks for saving me before it was too late. I'll be smarter the next time around.

Libby, New York

I'm not suggesting that some form of attraction isn't necessary. As a single, I enjoyed a good bout of infatuation as much as anyone. But before you commit your life to another person, don't you want to make sure the compatibility will last past the intense emotions?

So why not give yourself the best chance for a forever match?

1. Compare your families of origin.
2. Look at birth order.
3. Consider both of your personalities.
4. Take notes, then ask yourself, *Is this a good match on paper?*

If all of the above traits seem to be a "go," then delve into your potential partner's early childhood memories. Do they view the world as a safe place, a happy place, a dangerous place, or an evil place? Are they a controller, a pleaser, a charmer, or a victim?

Then ask yourself, *Is this really the kind of person I want to live with for the rest of my life? Is she working on becoming less of a victim? Is he working on becoming less of a controller? Is he using controlling tendencies for good causes (nursing, teaching) or bad (manipulating, terrorizing, politicking)?*

Once you understand your potential partner's early childhood memories, you also have good clues about what their rule book

225

looks like. You can then ask yourself, *Is this person's rule book compatible with mine?* By "compatible," I don't mean the same. No two rule books are exactly the same, because every person lives through different experiences, and even members of the same family view the same events differently. And, remember, same isn't always best.

By "compatible," here's what I mean. My wife, Sande, is willing to live with the fact that I'm a bit of a rule breaker, and I appreciate the fact that Sande would never break a rule. She brings order into my life; I bring a little fun into hers. Our rule books work well together, and neither Sande nor I ever try to change each other's rule book. We accept them as they are.

> *Most of us dream of marrying a giver. So why do so many people, women in particular, marry a taker?*

You should also use your own early childhood memories to help correct previous bad choices. For instance, I think most of us dream of marrying a giver. So why do so many people, women in particular, marry a taker?

If this is your story, step back and ask yourself the hard questions. Go ahead—no one's listening. Be brutally honest. When you dated that last taker for three and a half years, what did it get you? Stress with your other family members who saw the guy for what he was? Lack of time with people who really care about you and aren't interested in just using you? A broken heart? An abortion?

Then have a conversation that goes something like this: *I sort of gravitate toward those takers, don't I? I wonder why that is. You know, my mom did that too. As much as I hate to admit it, I'm an awful lot like her. That's scary. She's gone through three marriages. I don't want to do that.*

This is smart-decision time. Are you going to behave differently in the future? Are you going to delve into your memories so you understand your basic motivation? Will you be directed by responsible choices or swept off your feet by the next taker who is just a little more handsome, a little slicker, and a little more packaged than the last one? If this is a trouble area for you, I suggest that you read my book *Pleasers*.

Don't get me wrong; takers can be fun—for a while. But eventually, especially if you marry one, you'll be left alone. He'll be out bow hunting or bowling when you're left home changing diapers. When you're gripped with menstrual cramps, he'll be at the corner bar with his buddies or sitting in a recliner asking when dinner is going to be ready. If you truly want to hunt for a giver, stop acting like someone who is easily taken.

Lies You Tell Yourself

He gets angry only because he wants to protect me.
He wouldn't have done that if I hadn't made him mad.
He's always sorry . . . afterward.

Finally, look at your potential partner's capability to speak your love language. If you need a lot of time, you'll be miserable if you marry a driven, type A person who will always be too busy to fulfill the needs of your love language. If one of your primary goals is to live in a nice neighborhood and send all your kids to a private school, you might want to marry someone who can love you by providing the financial income necessary to afford all that. That means you'll have to sacrifice some of that person's time, conversation, and attention, but that won't matter so much if your love language is receiving gifts (within reason).

If you truly want to hunt for a giver, stop acting like someone who is easily taken.

When you marry someone, you're making a big commitment. To love that person for the rest of your life, yes—but also to meet their needs (and that includes their love language) for the rest of your life. If you can't stand the thought of a 30-minute heart-to-heart talk, why marry a person who will always want to be loved with words of affirmation or quality time?

When you look at a relationship this way, you're asking the kinds of questions that will lead to a compatible and lifelong union. And isn't that really what you want?

If You're Married . . .

If you're already married, you're standing with both feet in a pot of water. The temperature may be cool, just right, or a little too warm for comfort.

What if you didn't know about personality, birth order, early childhood memories, and the love languages before you got married? Are you in trouble? There's no need to get nervous—yet. Once the choice is made, you need to make the best of it, and you can if you're armed with the right information. (Note that I am *not* talking about situations of abuse—no woman or man should ever stay in a relationship where they are being abused in any way.) I know a number of happily married firstborn couples, for instance, who have beaten the odds and who have a very successful relationship. How have they done it?

Lee and Jamie, both firstborns, have been married for over 20 years. Both are hard-driving personalities, excellent in their careers. So how do they make it work? "We don't compete with each other," Jamie says. "I'm in the design field. Lee's in the engineering field. So we can both be the best at what we do without stepping on each other's toes."

"Yeah," Lee adds, "and because our fields are so different, we aren't even tempted to boss each other around."

They do the same thing at home—they keep their work responsibilities completely distinct. Lee cooks dinner, Jamie does the dishes. Jamie does the laundry, Lee mows the yard. Their biggest challenge, though, is making sure they set aside time just for the two of them since both work over 50 hours a week.

How can you have a successful marriage with someone of the same birth order?

The main thing is to be aware of your weaknesses, anticipate the fallout, and learn to act accordingly. For instance, two firstborns will most likely fight more than other couples because both are used to being in charge. Each needs to let the other person win now and then—even though doing so is completely foreign to a firstborn's traits. Each will also need to go out of their way to find different methods of serving their partner through their love language, rather than controlling or manipulating.

If two lastborns are married, the first thing they need to do is watch their spending habits. They may need to write up a budget or even visit a financial counselor. They'll have to learn to set a proper schedule for themselves and their children—even though doing so will seem constricting and weird. They'll also need to put the love languages to use, as both will tend to be self-centered.

If two middleborns are married, they'll get along great—as long as everything is moving along smoothly in their relationship.

> *Two firstborns will most likely fight more than other couples because both are used to being in charge. Each needs to let the other person win now and then.*

The problem comes when there's conflict, and conflict is an element of every marriage. If two stereotypical middle children want to avoid conflict, you don't have to have a PhD to figure out what's going to happen in the marriage. They'll both tend to sweep emotional issues under the rug rather than dealing with them. At such times, middleborns, who are peacemakers at heart, need to work hard at communicating their true thoughts and feelings—not just ones that will make each other feel good and not cause waves.

Understanding how each person in their family gives and receives love is very important for lastborns, who must learn how to focus on someone other than themselves.

You can also use your knowledge of the four basic personalities to work through personal disagreements. If you're a Standard

Poodle, you can learn to lighten up—not everyone has to read the newspaper from front to back just because you think that's the right way to do it. Let your Yorkie partner start with the comics or the sports page, and learn to choose your battles wisely.

If you're a Great Dane, understand that love is not about winning or doing things your way. It's about serving, cherishing others, and putting them first.

If you're an Irish Setter, you need to do the opposite of what I'm suggesting the Great Danes do. You need to assert yourself more and be more honest about your feelings. You need to talk about your desires, or else you risk falling into a smoldering resentment when you're overwhelmed by your partner's desires and never get your way.

If you're a Yorkie, realize that the world doesn't revolve around you. Other people are important too. Since looking after your own interests will come more naturally to you, work hard at listening to what your loved ones are really saying through their words and actions. Focus on meeting their needs in the specific way they want to be loved.

Exploring your spouse's childhood memories, as well as your own, will help you understand why your husband has a naive optimism or why your wife has taken years to start feeling safe in your relationship. You've married a person with a very influential past. For good or for ill, this past is part of your marriage, and it's perilous to ignore it. You can't rewrite your spouse's rule book—only they can do that, and only within certain parameters. What you can do is become more understanding of the mental processes your spouse goes through as they make decisions and respond to others.

When you discover your spouse's love language, you have the key to their heart. Learning to master that language will give you far more fulfillment than even being well loved yourself. It will make the new you a well-rounded person who is thoughtful, considerate, levelheaded, a loyal friend, and a passionate lover.

The New You at Work

Everything we've talked about in the Monday through Friday chapters can be readily applied in the workplace. For example, a salesperson could improve her sales remarkably if she would start approaching potential customers by considering their birth order.[1]

And you don't want to treat a firstborn boss the same way you'd treat a lastborn boss or a middleborn boss. The firstborn boss will probably want just the facts. He needs data to support his conclusions, and if you come in with an emotional appeal, you'll lose nine times out of ten. If you're trying to get through to a lastborn, however, you'll need to schmooze a little bit—but not in any way showing a lack of respect (lastborns are sensitive to not being respected). If you can effectively use humor, so much the better. Make your time with the lastborn enjoyable, and you'll increase your effectiveness with her more often than not.

And how can you best interact with a middleborn boss? Middleborns are the most entrepreneurial of the birth orders. Don't be afraid to voice your suggestions and your innovative ideas; you might find a very receptive boss. Loyalty is extremely important to middleborns, and they value a team-oriented approach and reward it.

Simply said, when you are interacting in a work environment (whether you work from home, in an office, on the field, or as a volunteer for community leadership), ask yourself, *Given this person's personality, what's the best way to interact with them?*

As you choose your vocation or consider a vocational change, put birth order to work for you. Most middleborns make excellent middle managers. They can be great assistant principals, and they may actually enjoy being an assistant principal more than becoming the senior principal. Protect yourself from being promoted to a position in which you won't be able to succeed.

Does this mean middleborn children are unfit to be CEOs and presidents? Of course not. Several past United States presidents were middleborn children. There are exceptions to every rule, due to each person's unique history and makeup.

But by using all four of the areas we've talked about in this book (personalities, birth orders, early childhood memories, and love languages), you can understand yourself far better, so you'll have a good idea of the types of jobs you'll be satisfied doing.

For example, while I know a successful accountant who is a lastborn, most lastborns—particularly if they're Yorkie by temperament—would be bored stiff as accountants. They need more interaction with people than the accounting profession usually provides.

Also consider your personality. If you're a Yorkie type, you may need to think twice about being self-employed, if self-employment will mean staying home by yourself and working in virtual isolation all day long. While some people revel in solitude (especially Irish Setters), others can't stand it.

Great Danes will have a difficult time taking orders from others. They usually won't enjoy a job that offers little personal freedom or that feels too constricting. Standard Poodles need time to think and reflect. Yorkies usually prefer a more relaxed environment. Irish Setters need to be in a workplace where they are trusted, they are asked for their opinion, and their input is valued on the team.

Take all these factors into consideration when you think about where you can be most successful.

In addition to considering personality and birth order, you can look to early childhood memories to both increase your performance and help you anticipate potential pitfalls. If your boss has a rule book in which rules are sacred just because they are rules, and your rule book states that rules are made to be broken, check your natural tendencies and do things by the book. You can drive five miles per hour over the speed limit as soon as you get out of the office, but you'd better not leave until the clock is firmly past 5:00. If your boss's rule book leads her to believe that the world

---

How My Life Changed

When our division was downsized, life in the office went from a normal chaos to stressful. Those of us who didn't get axed started reporting to a new manager. After day one, we were sure she was out to fire all of us. We were scared to even take a coffee break for fear she'd think we weren't working.

After two months like that, I was about ready to scream . . . or quit. Then you came and talked to our accounting group over lunch. Afterward, in a Q & A with our new manager, we all talked about birth order. I found out she was an only child, and all the personality traits started to make sense. I began to notice that she was even harder on herself than she was on us. One day her father came to visit, and I really got the picture. Talk about a perfectionist snob—he was. For the first time, I started to feel empathy for the woman I thought was my enemy.

Things in the office haven't lightened up a lot—my boss is still the same person—but I no longer take her hard-driving comments so personally. I know she's got her own issues to work out.

Thanks, Dr. L, for giving me some perspective.

Miranda, New Jersey

---

is a scary place, you should go out of your way to show her you're not a threat—you're on her side.

When you mess up, use your memories to provide you with clues as to why. Ask yourself, *Am I a bridge builder, or do I burn bridges? Do I burn bridges because I get mad when things don't go my way? Have I been too petty, too lazy, too irresponsible? Why might that be? And how can I change that?*

If I want to show appreciation for my boss or co-workers or subordinates, I'll use love languages since I recognize that different people value different methods of affirmation. For instance, during an evaluation I may offer several different bonuses for Christmas, maybe even letting people make their own choice: an extra day off, a new office chair, a round of golf, etc. If I know an employee is dying for words of affirmation, I'll put his name in the company newspaper and give him a big compliment. In other words, I won't treat everyone the same because I know they don't want to be affirmed the same way.

I can hear the naysayers already. "Come off it, Leman. How am I supposed to know my boss's birth order without looking like an idiot? Like I'm supposed to ask him that over his morning coffee? And for crying out loud, you must be joking when you talk about learning a subordinate's love language. That type of thinking would get me laughed out of the office or labeled as downright weird."

Not so fast. There's a simple tool you can use that's remarkably effective to reveal all we've talked about and more. It's inexpensive but highly efficient. It's called "conversation."

> *There's a simple tool you can use that's remarkably effective to reveal all we've talked about and more. It's inexpensive but highly efficient. It's called "conversation."*

I'm not suggesting you act like a shrink during a lunch or coffee break: "So, Susan, tell me your three earliest childhood memories. . . ." But you can intermingle comments with the group's analysis of the Buffalo Bills and Washington Redskins: "So, you went to the game with your brother? Is he older or younger?"

More often than not, the person you ask will usually give you his full birth order: "He's my older brother. There's just the two of us."

When the group gets together just to talk, go quietly about your secret mission. Listen for clues about rule books. Is one man always ridiculing the type of people who toe the party line? Is another woman upset because people don't obey the recommended speed limit sign on the curve just a mile north of the office?

Pay attention to what people complain about. Do they feel overworked? Underappreciated? Undercompensated? You don't need to quiz someone to find out these things. They're usually out for display, in full color.

Personality is pretty easy to pick up on if you take a few minutes to think about the people you know. It doesn't take a doctorate to tell a Yorkie from a Standard Poodle—just listen to who laughs more! A Great Dane will be involved in most of the politicking, and the Standard Poodle will love to pass out ten-page memos on the correct use of the copy machine, while the Irish Setter will try to smooth the waters and help everyone just get along.

In short, I'm asking you to take a sincere interest in the people you work with. Get to know them. Find out what motivates them. Take your eyes off yourself for a few minutes and learn to look at the world through their eyes.

It's Up to You

As you gain a better understanding of others and begin to show more consideration of them, you will also gain a deeper understanding and a healthy appreciation of yourself. You will no longer believe the lies that your private logic is whispering to you. You won't unload the dump truck of manure on yourself when things go wrong. You'll begin to see life and people in a much more balanced perspective.

You'll accept yourself, boost your confidence, and change your life—in just five days!

And when you do so, you'll go much further than you ever dreamed possible in *all* aspects of your life—in your relationships and in your work life.

You'll accept yourself, boost your confidence, and change your life—in just five days!

The Top Ten Countdown to Having a New You by Friday

10. Pinpoint the area(s) you want to change about yourself.
9. Decide that you're not just going to *try* to become a new you this time. You're going to *do* it.
8. Identify your personality and all its strengths and weaknesses.
7. Identify your birth order and all its strengths and weaknesses.
6. Identify your three earliest memories and evaluate what they say about you and your private logic.
5. Identify the lies you tell yourself—and refuse to believe them.
4. Identify your primary love language—and those of your friends and family members.
3. Decide how you need to act differently in your relationships—and then do it.
2. Decide how you need to act differently in your work—and then do it.
1. Give yourself a break. Everyone messes up sometimes. Each day's a new day.

Notes

Introduction: This Book Ought to Cost $199

1. Paul Aurandt, *More of Paul Harvey's The Rest of the Story* (New York: William Morrow & Co., 1980), 111–12.
2. Ibid.

Monday: Just Who Do You Think You Are?

1. Peter Johnson, "Gumbel's Guffaw," *USA Today*, November 8, 1999.
2. "Bloodletting & the Four Humors," Collect Medical Antiques, January 9, 2010, http://www.collectmedicalantiques.com/bloodletting.html.
3. Ibid.
4. Ibid.
5. Ibid.

Tuesday: Maybe You Do Belong in the Zoo!

1. For more on birth order, see Kevin Leman, *The Birth Order Book* (Grand Rapids: Revell, 2009).
2. For more on this subject, see chapters 2 and 3 in Leman, *Birth Order Book*.
3. Kevin Leman, *Why Your Best Is Good Enough* (Grand Rapids: Revell, 2010).

Bonus Section for the Curious: Who's Who?

1. Answers to "Guess Who?"
For more on why I categorize these famous folks the way I do, see *The Birth Order Book*. (For instance, Steve Martin is technically a lastborn—at least in ordinal position in the family—so why do I put him in the firstborn camp? You'll know after you read *The Birth Order Book*.)

Only children	*Middle children*
Barack Obama	George Bush Sr.
Robert De Niro	Dwight Eisenhower
Laurence Fishburne	Grover Cleveland
Anthony Hopkins	John F. Kennedy
James Earl Jones	Richard Nixon
Tommy Lee Jones	Donald Trump
Firstborns	*Lastborns or babies*
Hillary Clinton	Eddie Murphy
Steve Martin (lastborn in his family,	Martin Short
but the firstborn son)	Ellen DeGeneres
Bill Cosby	Whoopi Goldberg
Harrison Ford	Jay Leno
Matthew Perry	Stephen Colbert
Jennifer Aniston	Steve Carell
Angelina Jolie	Jon Stewart
Brad Pitt	Billy Crystal
Chuck Norris	Danny DeVito
Sylvester Stallone	Drew Carey
Reese Witherspoon	Jim Carrey
Ben Affleck	Chevy Chase
Oprah Winfrey	Ronald Reagan

2. For more on why this is true, see Kevin Leman, *Pleasers* (Grand Rapids: Revell, 2006). This book is being reissued by the publisher as *Smart Women Know When to Say No* in December 2010.

3. Quotes and information about Oprah Winfrey are taken from the following sources: Maya Angelou, "How Oprah's Changed Our World," *McCall's*, November 1998, 67; Emma Bland, "Battle of the Bulge," *McCall's*, November 1998, 68; Lynette Clemetson, "Oprah on Oprah" and "It Is a Constant Work," *Newsweek*, January 8, 2001, 45; Deirdre Donahue, "Live Your Best Life, with Oprah," *USA Today*, July 2, 2001; "Oprah Encourages Roosevelt University Grads to Find Their Calling in Life During Commencement Address," *Jet*, June 19, 2000; Joanna Powell, "Oprah's Awakening," *Good Housekeeping*, December 1998, 209; Lisa Russell and Cindy Dampier, "Oprah Winfrey," *People*, March 15, 1999, 22; Ron Stodghill, "Daring to Go There," *Time*, October 5, 1998, 80; Oprah Winfrey, "The Courage to Dream," *Essence*, December 1998, 149.

4. For more on the subject of firstborns, see Kevin Leman, *Born to Win* (Grand Rapids: Revell, 2009).

5. Dominic Wills, "Robert De Niro," Robert De Niro website, http://www.westlord .com/robertdeniro/eng-bio.html (accessed January 23, 2010).

6. Ibid., http://www.westlord.com/robertdeniro/eng-quotes.html (accessed January 23, 2010).

7. Ibid,

8. Other quotes and information about Robert De Niro are taken from the following sources: "Biography for Robert De Niro," The Internet Movie Database, http://www

.imdb.com/name/nm0000134/bio (accessed January 23, 2010); "Robert De Niro," Robert De Niro website, http://www.westlord.com/robertdeniro/eng-home.html (accessed January 23, 2010); "Robert De Niro," Thespian Net, http://www.thespiannet .com/actors/D/deniro_robert/robert_deniro.shtml (accessed January 23, 2010); "Robert De Niro Biography," Bio, http://www.thebiographychannel.co.uk/biographies/robert-de-niro.html (accessed January 23, 2010); "Robert De Niro Biography," WhoABC, http://www.whoabc.com/men/r/robert-de-niro (accessed January 23, 2010); "Robert De Niro—Rotten Tomatoes Celebrity Profile," Rotten Tomatoes, http://www.rotten to matoes.com/celebrity/robert_de_niro/biography/php (accessed January 23, 2010).

9. James Wolcott, "Letterman Unbound," *New Yorker*, June 3, 1996, 82.

10. Ibid.

11. Other quotes and information about Jay Leno and Dave Letterman are taken from the following sources: Bill Carter, *The Late Shift: Letterman, Leno, and the Network Battle for the Night* (New York: Hyperion, 1994); Tom Gliatto, "Fade to Black," *People*, October 26, 1998; Lloyd Grove, "Late-Night Sweats," *Vanity Fair*, October 1996, 176; David Handelman, "Dave's Real World," *Vogue*, January 1995, 78; Fred Schruers, "Dave vs. Dave," *Rolling Stone*, May 30, 1996, 30; Wolcott, "Letterman Unbound," 82; Bill Zehme, "Letterman Lets His Guard Down," *Esquire*, December 1994, 98.

12. Nancy Schimelpfening, "Jim Carrey," About.com, April 17, 2006, http://depres sion.about.com/od/famous/p/jimcarrey.htm.

13. Kassidy Emmerson, "Little Known Facts about Jim Carrey," July 18, 2007, http:// www.associatedcontent.com/article/309765/little_known_facts_about_jim_carrey .htm.

14. Other quotes and information about Jim Carrey are taken from the following sources: "Actors—Jim Carrey," eBay, http://listing-index.ebay.com/actors/Jim_Carrey .html (accessed January 21, 2010); Emmerson, "Little Known Facts"; "Jim Carrey—Biography," TalkTalk, http://www.talktalk.co.uk/entertainment/film/biography/artist/ jim-carrey/biography/53 (accessed January 21, 2010); "Jim Carrey Online: FAQ," http:// www.jimcarreyonline.com/forum/jcofaq.php (accessed January 21, 2010); Schimelp fening, "Jim Carrey."

Wednesday: Oh, the Lies We Tell . . . Ourselves

1. Casey Stengel, quoted in Michael Bamberger, "Dom DiMaggio," *Sports Illustrated*, July 2, 2001, 105.

2. Dom DiMaggio, quoted in Bamberger, "Dom DiMaggio," 106.

3. Dan Vergano, "Mind Makes Memories Fonder—but False," *USA Today*, July 2, 2001.

4. Ibid.

5. Ibid.

6. Ibid.

7. "John Daly Weight Loss: Before and After Photos," *The Huffington Post*, December 9, 2009, http://www.huffingtonpost.com/2009/12/08/john-daly-weight-loss-bef_n_384759.html.

8. Mark Seal, "Still Afloat," *Golf Digest*, August 2001, 99.

9. Ibid., 108.

10. For more on the styles of parenting, see Kevin Leman, *Have a New Kid by Friday* (Grand Rapids: Revell, 2008).

11. Andy Seiler, "Lemmon Was Just One of Us," *USA Today*, June 29, 2001.

12. Jack Lemmon, quoted in Seiler, "Lemmon Was Just One of Us."

13. Donahue, "Live Your Best Life."

Thursday: How Do You Spell "Love"?

1. Dr. Gary Chapman, *The Five Love Languages: How to Express Heartfelt Commitment to Your Mate* (Chicago: Northfield Publishing, 1992), 106.

2. To understand what men are really looking for, see Kevin Leman, *Have a New Husband by Friday* (Grand Rapids: Revell, 2009).

3. Dr. Harry Schaumburg, *False Intimacy: Understanding the Struggle of Sexual Addiction* (Colorado Springs: NavPress, 1997), 175–76.

4. For more on why it's important to make love outside the bedroom, see Kevin Leman, *Sex Begins in the Kitchen* (Grand Rapids: Revell, 2006) and *Turn Up the Heat* (Grand Rapids: Revell, 2009).

5. For more on this, see Leman, *Birth Order Book*.

Friday: Shrink Thyself

1. David Wild, "Steve Martin: The Rolling Stone Interview," *Rolling Stone*, September 2, 1999.

2. This and many other details are taken from "Steve Martin," *Current Biography*, November 2000, 385; David Wild, "Steve Martin," 88.

3. "Steve Martin," *Current Biography*, 385.

4. Chuck Arnold, "Chatter," *People*, August 30, 1999, 146.

5. R. J. Smith, "Steve Martin, in Revision," *New York Times Magazine*, August 8, 1999, 28.

6. Ibid.

7. Ibid.

8. Ibid., 29.

9. Ibid.

10. Bernard Weinraub, "The Wiser Guy," *McCall's*, September 1999, 38.

11. Cathleen Fillmore, "The Houdini of Jailbirds," *The Globe and Mail*, June 23, 2001.

12. If you want to see change in your home with your kids, you can do it in just five days with my book *Have a New Kid by Friday*.

13. Morris Walker, *Steve Martin: The Magic Years* (New York: S.P.I. Books, 2001), 272–73.

14. Graydon Carter, "Easy Does It," *Vanity Fair*, February 2001, 38.

Bonus Section for the Curious: How the New You Works

1. For more on how birth order affects work, particularly the sales occupation, see Leman, *Birth Order Book*.

About Dr. Kevin Leman

An internationally known psychologist, humorist, radio and television personality, and speaker, Dr. Kevin Leman has taught and entertained audiences worldwide with his wit and commonsense psychology.

Dr. Leman is the *New York Times* bestselling and award-winning author of over 35 books about marriage and family issues, including *Have a New Kid by Friday*, *The Birth Order Book*, *Have a New Husband by Friday*, *Making Children Mind without Losing Yours*, *Sex Begins in the Kitchen*, and *Sheet Music*. He has made thousands of house calls for radio and television programs, including *Fox & Friends*, *The View*, Fox's *The Morning Show*, *Today*, *Oprah*, CBS's *The Early Show*, *Janet Parshall's America*, *Live with Regis Philbin*, CNN's *American Morning*, *Life Today* with James Robison, and *Focus on the Family*. Dr. Leman has also served as a contributing family psychologist to *Good Morning America*.

He is coauthor with his son, Kevin Leman II, of a series of illustrated children's books for each child in the family. He is also featured on eight video series on marriage, parenting, blended families, and single parenting. He is the founder and president of

Couples of Promise, an organization designed and committed to helping couples remain happily married, and is a founding faculty member of iQuestions.com.

Dr. Leman's professional affiliations include the American Psychological Association, the American Federation of Television and Radio Artists, and the North American Society of Adlerian Psychology.

In 1993, he was the recipient of the Distinguished Alumnus Award of North Park University in Chicago. In 2003, he received from the University of Arizona the highest award that a university can extend to its own: the Alumni Achievement Award.

Dr. Leman attended North Park University. He received his bachelor's degree in psychology from the University of Arizona, where he later earned his master's and doctorate degrees. Originally from Williamsville, New York, he and his wife, Sande, live in Tucson, Arizona. They have five children and two grandchildren.

For information regarding speaking availability, business consultations, seminars, or the annual Couples of Promise cruise, please contact:

Dr. Kevin Leman
P.O. Box 35370
Tucson, Arizona 85740
Phone: (520) 797-3830
Fax: (520) 797-3809
www.drleman.com

Resources by Dr. Kevin Leman

Books for Adults

Have a New Kid by Friday

Have a New Husband by Friday

Have a New You by Friday

The Birth Order Book

Under the Sheets

Sheet Music

Making Children Mind without Losing Yours

Born to Win

Sex Begins in the Kitchen

7 Things He'll Never Tell You . . . But You Need to Know

What Your Childhood Memories Say about You

Running the Rapids

What a Difference a Daddy Makes

The Way of the Shepherd (written with William Pentak)

Home Court Advantage

Becoming the Parent God Wants You to Be

Becoming a Couple of Promise

A Chicken's Guide to Talking Turkey with Your Kids about Sex (written with Kathy Flores Bell)

First-Time Mom

Keeping Your Family Strong in a World Gone Wrong

Step-parenting 101

The Perfect Match

Be Your Own Shrink

*Say Good-bye to Stress**

Single Parenting That Works

Why Your Best Is Good Enough

Pleasers[†]

Books for Children, with Kevin Leman II

My Firstborn, There's No One Like You

My Middle Child, There's No One Like You

My Youngest, There's No One Like You

My Only Child, There's No One Like You

My Adopted Child, There's No One Like You

My Grandchild, There's No One Like You

DVD/Video Series

Have a New Kid by Friday

*This book is being reissued by the publisher as *Stopping Stress before It Stops You* in April 2011.

†This book is being reissued by the publisher as *Smart Women Know When to Say No* in December 2010.

246

Making Children Mind without Losing Yours (Christian—parenting edition)

Making Children Mind without Losing Yours (Mainstream—public school teacher edition)

Value-Packed Parenting

Making the Most of Marriage

Running the Rapids

Single Parenting That Works

Bringing Peace and Harmony to the Blended Family

Available at 1-800-770-3830 or www.drleman.com

Take the
5-Day Challenge

Family expert Dr. Kevin Leman reveals in this *New York Times* bestseller why your kids do what they do and what you can do about it—in just five days!

Have a New Husband by <u>Friday</u>?
Is that even possible?

Dr. Kevin Leman says it is. The *New York Times* bestselling author and relationship expert shows you how with his easy and accessible principles.

Find Out How Your Birth Order
Influences the Way You React to Your World

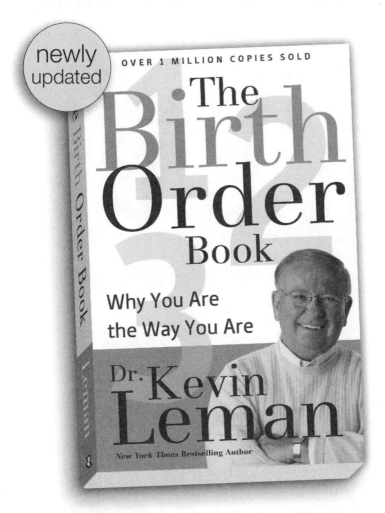

newly updated

OVER 1 MILLION COPIES SOLD

The Birth Order Book

Why You Are the Way You Are

Dr. Kevin Leman

New York Times Bestselling Author

Firstborn? Only child? Middle child? Baby of the family? Find out what your birth order means to you, your relationships, and your career in this updated edition of the bestselling book.

Kid-tested,
Parent-approved

If anyone understands why children behave the way they do, it's Dr. Kevin Leman. In this bestseller, he equips parents with seven principles of "reality discipline"—a loving, no-nonsense parenting approach that really works.

Break free
from perfectionism!

Are you an expert at finding flaws within yourself? Do you tend to procrastinate, set unrealistic goals, or continually try to please others?

**If you want to make a positive change in your life,
this is the place to start.**